# Knoxville Music before Bluegrass

IMAGES of America

Geographical regions may be the single greatest contributing factor to the music that has come from Tennessee. This book is dedicated to those regions defined as Southern Appalachia in East Tennessee, the Cumberland River Valley of Middle Tennessee, and the Mississippi Delta of West Tennessee. It was in the Southern Appalachian area of West Virginia, Virginia, and East Tennessee that the author learned to play banjo and discovered the music called bluegrass. It was in the Cumberland River Valley of Kentucky, Middle Tennessee, and Nashville that the author completed much of his formal education and learned to appreciate the songwriters and craft of country music and the business of music. It was in the Mississippi Delta area of West Tennessee that the author embraced the blues and learned to celebrate the diversity of peoples that make this rich music possible. (Author's collection.)

ON THE COVER: The fiddle is the instrument most identified with the migration of tunes and ballads from Ireland, Scotland, Wales, and England to Appalachia. Along with banjo, mandolin, guitar, and bass, the violin became the foundation for string band, hillbilly, and later, bluegrass music. (LOC.)

IMAGES
*of America*

# KNOXVILLE MUSIC BEFORE BLUEGRASS

Tim Sharp

ARCADIA
PUBLISHING

Copyright © 2020 by Tim Sharp
ISBN 978-1-4671-0435-7

Published by Arcadia Publishing
Charleston, South Carolina

Library of Congress Control Number: 2019943158

For all general information, please contact Arcadia Publishing:
Telephone 843-853-2070
Fax 843-853-0044
E-mail sales@arcadiapublishing.com
For customer service and orders:
Toll-Free 1-888-313-2665

Visit us on the Internet at www.arcadiapublishing.com

*The inspiration, motivation, and interest in the topic of the folk and popular music of Tennessee is enhanced by collaborators Wes Ramsay, Timothy Michael Powell, the Chuck Nation Band, Jane and Emma Jane, and musicians who share a passion for this music.*

# Contents

| | | |
|---|---|---|
| Acknowledgments | | 6 |
| Introduction | | 7 |
| 1. | United States of Tennessee | 9 |
| 2. | Wexford Girl Becomes the Knoxville Girl | 29 |
| 3. | Read the Bible, Pray, Give Thanks, and Play Fiddle | 41 |
| 4. | The Lonesome Valley | 55 |
| 5. | Cultures Collide, Creating a New Art Form | 63 |
| 6. | The Grass Is Bluer on the Other Side | 73 |
| 7. | A High Lonesome Sound | 85 |
| 8. | Stars Align | 95 |
| 9. | Appalachia Takes to the Air | 99 |
| 10. | What Makes Bluegrass Bluegrass? | 101 |
| Bibliography | | 125 |
| Index | | 127 |

# Acknowledgments

The images included in *Knoxville Music before Bluegrass* tell their own story of the evolving nature of a musical genre that emerged from solo fiddle tunes and mountain ballads to become the ensemble music now known as bluegrass. The pictures and illustrations on the following pages are not so much explicit examples of the story being told as they are meant to be impressions hinting at the component parts of this narrative. This style of illustration was also used in the author's two other books in this series, *Nashville Music before Country* and *Memphis Music before the Blues*.

The author has chosen to structure *Knoxville Music before Bluegrass* in this manner for practical and poetic reasons. The practical reason is that photography was not invented until later in the history of this music, so to fill that gap, pertinent images, sketches, maps, and landscapes in the early chapters are meant to spark the imagination as well as illustrate the developing story. Poetic choices come from the fact that music is an ephemeral art form existing more in the world of sound than sight. Once again, the imagination has to be called upon to fill some gaps. The hope is that the reader, with guidance from the narrative, can help form some of the necessary mental pictures that tell this story. Throughout the book, many remarkable images document the recipe of how bluegrass music was created from various converging ingredients.

Images in this book appear courtesy of the English Folk Dance & Song Society, London, England (EFD); National Portrait Gallery, London, England (NPG); Archives of Appalachia, Eastern Tennessee State University, Johnson City, Tennessee (AOA); Tennessee State Library and Archives, Nashville, Tennessee (TSL); Center for Popular Music, Middle Tennessee State University, Murfreesboro, Tennessee (CPM); Tennessee State Library and Archives, Nashville, Tennessee (TSL); Library of Congress, Washington, DC (LOC); the private hymnal collection of Dr. Richard Shadinger, Nashville, TN (RS); sketches from F.D. Srygley's 1891 publication *Seventy Years in Dixie* (FDS); and the private collections of Paula and Steve Bedell (PSB), Kevin Fore (KF), Charles Nation (CN), Patricia O'Neal (PO), Lindsay Alexander Owen (LAO), and Amanda Janette Sharp (AJS). Unless otherwise attributed, additional images appear courtesy of the author's private collection.

# INTRODUCTION

*Knoxville Music before Bluegrass* is the story of the early music that existed in the same region of the United States that gave birth to country music and bluegrass. Bluegrass music as a genre came into being near the midpoint of the 20th century. The art form as a subgenre of its parent, country music, is just barely older than the emergence of Elvis Presley and the Beatles. Country music came of age only slightly earlier, in the first quarter of the 20th century.

Similar to the two earlier publications in this series, *Memphis Music before the Blues* and *Nashville Music before Country*, *Knoxville Music before Bluegrass* completes the series of three pictorial histories that document the music-making that was taking place in Knoxville and East Tennessee before the rise of the iconic music for which these regions are now internationally recognized.

Country and bluegrass are the products of commercial and professional artistic enterprise. Recording companies such as RCA Victor and OKeh Records made the regional music that came from East Tennessee and the Southern Appalachian region available to a national audience through recording and mass media broadcasts. Regional artists grew in popularity as their music was heard thanks to record sales and radio broadcasts.

Over the quarter century that followed the Bristol, Tennessee, recording sessions of 1927 known as the "Big Bang" of country music, this newly congealed genre embraced a range of traditions including British and Appalachian American ballads, wilderness and African American spirituals and gospel songs, vaudeville and minstrel songs, cowboy and western songs, blues, and swing. Bill Monroe and his Blue Grass Boys made their Grand Ole Opry premiere in 1939, and by 1950, Monroe and his band had crystallized the new genre that would be forever known as bluegrass.

It is enlightening to ponder the environment before the commercial industry came to embrace this music in terms of both the music and the way of life in the Appalachian mountain area of East Tennessee. In chapter three, we learn of these mountain conditions in the words of pioneering "songcatchers" Cecil Sharp and Maud Karpeles as they made their way through Southern Appalachia, meticulously recording some vivid observations in their diaries.

*Knoxville Music before Bluegrass* offers a glimpse into what Cecil Sharp described in his diary as an entire region that, at the turn of the 20th century, was still "isolated and protected from outside influence"—a description that includes the music of these people in its Appalachian mountain incubator before the world would come to know country music and bluegrass.

The narrative continues with images selected from the thousands of possible instrumental and vocal combinations that explored new ways of transmitting those mountain ballads in ever-evolving sounds. *Knoxville Music before Bluegrass* is about the storytelling through song that began with the migrated ballads of Scotland, Ireland, Wales, and England, and continued through the high lonesome sounds of Appalachian singers and ensembles that led to today's bluegrass.

The miracle of the music of Tennessee occurs in the alchemy of a particular people and vocabulary ("Appalachian"), defined by mountain isolation ("lonesome"), a unique heritage ("Scotch-Irish" and "African"), and coming of age in a perfect convergence of interest, photography, publication, recording, and broadcasting.

# One

# UNITED STATES OF TENNESSEE

On January 2, 2002, the US Treasury released the Tennessee coin for the quarter dollar. On that coin are three stars, representing the three geographical regions of West, Middle, and East Tennessee. Also depicted are three instruments: the guitar, the fiddle, and the trumpet. The trumpet represents W.C. Handy and the music of the blues of Memphis in the western part of the state; the guitar represents the country music industry that gained popularity in Middle Tennessee and Nashville through the WSM-produced shows of the Grand Ole Opry; and the fiddle represents the folk, mountain and bluegrass music of Bristol, Kingsport, Johnson City, and Knoxville in East Tennessee—truly, the music that existed in the mountains before all the other music the state is known for came into being.

From its earliest days, Tennessee has been a state with separate regions as well as musical "states of mind." In 1835, the state government established a supreme court with three judges, one each from East, Middle, and West Tennessee. Today, the state flag features three stars—one for each of these three distinct regions.

To observers of American popular music, the state of Tennessee appears to be something of a musical miracle. How is it possible that the beginnings of so many forms of American popular music can be traced to Tennessee? What is the story behind this musical miracle and its specific location within the lines of West, Middle, and East Tennessee? (AOA.)

*Knoxville Music before Bluegrass* is the story of the culture and the music that existed in the Appalachian region of East Tennessee long before new genres were born in the forms of bluegrass and country music. Although bluegrass music rightfully belongs to an entire region, not a specific city or state, no other region throughout the Appalachian South can claim a historic capital, or center, like East Tennessee can in the city of Knoxville. (LOC.)

Native peoples occupied Appalachia for at least 10,000 years, leaving a lasting imprint on its history and culture. The name Appalachia itself is thought to be Algonquian. In West Virginia, the area of Seneca Rocks reflects Seneca influence. In East Tennessee, tribute is paid to Sequoyah, the inventor of the Cherokee alphabet that is still in use today. The name *Tennessee* is taken from the Cherokee. (LOC.)

The Scotch-Irish people who arrived in Appalachia during the 18th century followed the Great Wagon Road, now the path of Interstate 81. This large area of Virginia was the gateway that German, French, and English immigrants had followed, taking land from the native population without any formal treaty. They spread into the Cumberland and Allegheny Plateaus in the early 1800s, harvesting the lumber and later mining the underground coal. (LOC.)

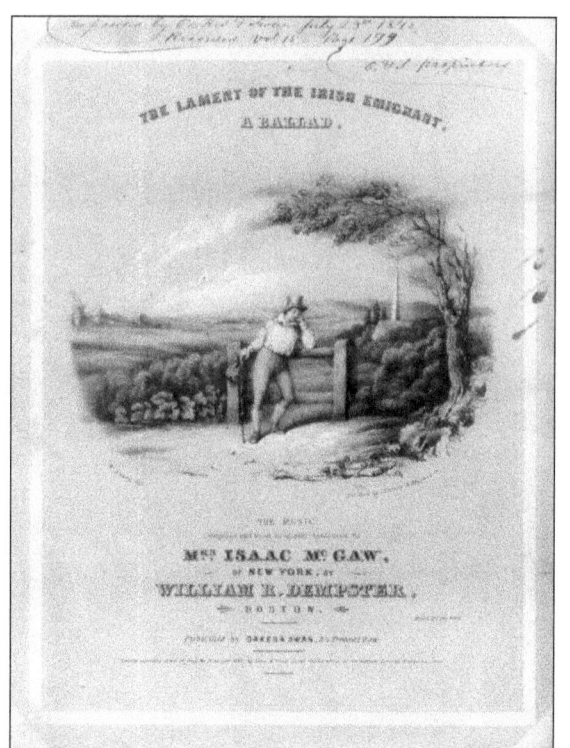

The immigration of the people known as Celts—Scotch-Irish, Ulster, Scots, Welsh, and English—to East Tennessee and the American South was considerable between the early 17th and late 18th centuries. Contemporary writers spoke of many people leaving Ireland and the Highlands of Scotland for the New World. (LOC.)

The story of the music of East Tennessee and *Knoxville Music before Bluegrass* starts in the early days of European immigration to the New World and can be traced back to the fiddle music and song ballads of Ireland, Scotland, and England that accompanied these early immigrants to the Appalachian region of eastern Tennessee. According to Irish journalist Billy Kennedy, about one in five Tennesseans can trace their roots back to the Scotch-Irish settlers of 250 years ago. (LOC.)

One of the attributes that makes East Tennessee unique throughout Appalachia is the presence of a capital city at the edge of the mountains—Knoxville. Southeastern Kentucky, western North Carolina, northern Georgia, and southwestern Virginia are very similar to eastern Tennessee. Knoxville typified the ethos of the Appalachian South and also provided a distinctive regional difference from its sister Tennessee regional music centers in Memphis and Nashville. (LOC.)

Knoxville became the center of population for this area of Appalachia after the arrival of Caucasian settlers in the late 18th century. Before this arrival, the area was dominated by the Cherokee and other native tribes who had established towns on the Little Tennessee River, approximately 40 miles south of the present-day city of Knoxville. (AJS.)

The major early influences in the area came from the native Cherokee people, and the British and French both claimed the area before 1763. Most of the intermingling that took place between the cultures and people was via traders in search of furs. By leasing, purchasing, and stealing land from the Cherokee, settlers began taking hold of the territory. (LOC.)

"Overhill people" was a nickname for the Cherokee people and others located in the historic settlements on the west side of the Appalachian Mountains of East Tennessee. The nickname was used by 18th-century European traders and explorers, as they had to cross the mountains, going "over the hills," to reach the settlements located along the lower Little Tennessee, Tellico, and Hiwassee Rivers. Overhill towns were consistently courted by British and French emissaries as the two powers struggled to control the lucrative fur trade. (LOC.)

The Overhill town of Tanasi was the capital of the Cherokee nation from 1721 to 1730 and became the namesake for the state of Tennessee. Chota, Tennessee, was later recognized as the Cherokee capital for most of the 18th century, when it was the major settlement. Many prominent Cherokee leaders were from Overhill towns such as Chota. Chota is now underwater as a result of Tennessee Valley Authority lake and dam development.

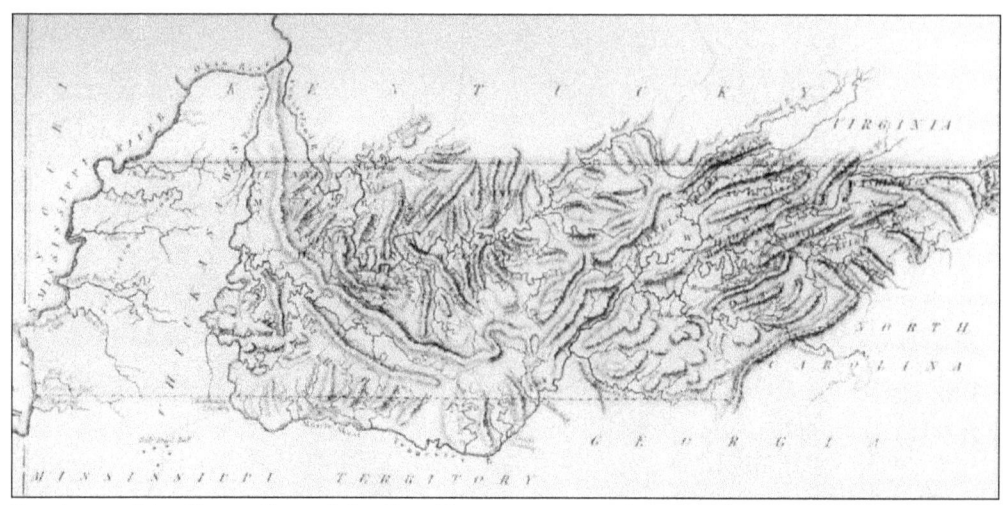

Residents of the Knoxville and the East Tennessee region lived by themselves for generations, walled in by natural barriers that made transportation to and from the area limited and difficult. Due to this isolation, Knoxville grew to become the cultural, commercial, and social capital of the area, attracting artisans who enlarged the status of the city even further. (TSL.)

Eastern Tennessee, with its mountains, rivers, timberland, and lakes, is similar in its geographical makeup to Scotland and Ireland, including in terms of its greenery. Many of the vistas familiar to immigrants from Ireland and Scotland were present in the landscape of the Southern Appalachians. (TSL.)

The main reasons for the emigration from Ireland and Scotland were unbearable living conditions. People left their homes for the promise, or hope, of a chance to continue the farming way of life they had enjoyed in Europe. The desire for land, better prices, fair treatment, unrestricted farming, reasonable tariffs, and an encouraging future were among the reasons people left their homes and countries. (LOC.)

The author's maternal grandmother and grandfather were born and grew up in this region of the country. Mollie Elizabeth Rowlett (born January 25, 1897) married Garrett Hobert Estep (born August 5, 1896) on December 19, 1915. They had thirteen children, with the author's mother being born in the middle—she was their seventh child and one of ten daughters. "Lizzie," as she was known by family and friends, was pregnant for almost 10 years of her life. (PO.)

Typical of the farm families and blue-collar inhabitants of the area, the Rowlett family owned a 300-acre farm that bordered the Tennessee and Virginia line. The back of the farm was in Claiborne County, Tennessee, and the front of the farm was in Lee County, Virginia. Just through Cumberland Gap, Tennessee, and a few miles north of the farm was the Kentucky state line and the Tri-State Peak. (PO.)

The author's maternal grandmother, Elizabeth "Lizzie" Rowlett Estep, said her father, "Pap," played the fiddle at all the local community gatherings when he was young. Fiddle-playing was a typical valued skill within a rural community and went hand in hand with communal life and social gatherings. It is common to see a photograph of an Appalachian family with a family member holding a fiddle or other mountain instrument, such as a guitar or banjo. (LAO.)

The Rowlett children grew up in a white frame house that had a parlor, dining room, large family room/bedroom, and kitchen, with bedrooms on the second floor. They were farmers, and as such, they were self-sufficient providers for their families. Floyd Rowlett, Lizzie Rowlett's father (and the author's great-grandfather), was a farmer, blacksmith, and part-owner of the only general store in the community, the Rowlett General Store. Lizzie met Hobert Estep during a Sunday school "march" at their church. Hobert was born in a log house in Frog Level (Ewing), Virginia, where he had been raised by his aunt and uncle after the death of his father. Hobert and Lizzie eloped and were married on December 19, 1915. Hobert worked for the Louisville & Nashville (L&N) Railroad as an assistant foreman for the bridge department in eastern Kentucky and later relocated to Corbin, Kentucky. Pictured above is John Estep in front of the Estep store in Harrogate, Tennessee; pictured below are Wiley (left), John (center), and Hobert Estep. (Below, PO.)

The author's father's side of the family took a different path into the Appalachian South. Rather than going through the Cumberland Gap, they followed the route of the Tennessee River to northern Alabama, an area on the western end of Appalachia. Strolling through the Clement-Delap family cemetery in a northern Alabama county that borders Tennessee, one is reminded that this story is only a few generations removed from today. Among those buried there are the author's great-great-great-grandmother Mary H. Phillips Smith and great-great-grandparents Stephen and Sarah Jane Smith Delap Clement. Sarah Jane's father, Sterling Smith of Lunenburg County, Virginia, died on August 28, 1828, eight months before she was born. Sarah and her widowed mother, Mary, and other family members began the move from Virginia through Tennessee to north Alabama when Sarah was three years old. (LOC.)

Several things may have inspired Mary Smith to move to Alabama with her family after Sterling Smith's death. In 1819, Virginia was becoming overpopulated, and Alabama had recently become the 22nd state. Additionally, cotton was the new cash crop in Alabama, so the promise of inexpensive, fertile land was alluring. This pioneering spirit and developmental drive had been passed down through Mary Smith's ancestral line. Mary's great-great-grandfather William Mayo (the author's seventh great-grandfather) was an English civil engineer who laid out the cities of Richmond and Petersburg, Virginia, and surveyed the line between North Carolina and Virginia. Mayo came to Virginia by way of Barbados in 1723. His father, Joseph Mayo (born c. 1691), was from Poulshot, Wiltshire, England.

The route Mary and Sarah Smith and other family members took to their new home near the Alabama–Tennessee border was along the same path taken by hundreds before and after them. It is family tradition that they traveled by oxcart along the Great Valley Wagon Road into Tennessee. Others, such as Daniel Boone and Davy Crockett, took the Cumberland Gap route, following the Cumberland River. After arriving in Tennessee, some travelers settled in the Watauga or Holston Valleys. Others boarded flat-bottomed riverboats and followed the same route as John Donelson along the Holston, Tennessee, Ohio, and Cumberland Rivers. The Smith party, however, departed the Tennessee River at Cottonport, Alabama, near present-day Decatur. Other Smith ancestors stopped and settled near the Cumberland Gap area in eastern Kentucky. (LOC.)

In mid-June 1776, a five-man committee, which included Thomas Jefferson, John Adams, and Benjamin Franklin, was tasked with drafting a formal statement of the colonies' intentions. In Philadelphia, Congress formally adopted the Declaration of Independence—largely written by Jefferson—on July 4, now celebrated as the birthdate of the United States. The literature of Northern Ireland goes to some length to identify the men of Ulster, Ireland, who signed the Declaration of Independence. There were at least eight, including Charles Thompson, secretary of the Continental Congress and native of the County Londonderry. Contemporary accounts also list the Irish involved in the printing of the original document and a considerable number who led during the defining battle of King's Mountain during the American Revolution. The Scotch and Ulster Irish would continue their influence in all matters of statesmanship as well as music and culture. (NPG.)

Most Ulster immigrants settled on the frontier line in New England and Pennsylvania, then moved south through the valleys of the great chain of the Appalachian Mountains into Virginia, Kentucky, the Carolinas, Tennessee, northern Georgia, and northern Alabama. This is the region that is now known for maintaining and developing a folk music tradition that would become country and bluegrass music. (LOC.)

On June 1, 1796, twenty years after the signing of the Declaration of Independence, Tennessee became the 16th state. The war for independence had decimated North Carolina, and many of the mountain settlers, such as the Wataugans, who were fiercely Scotch-Irish in origin and temperament, remained fiery and independent in their thinking. As North Carolina imposed tariffs on these settlers, they refused to comply and moved toward new statehood as early as 1784 in what was then the western part of the state. This would become the new state of Tennessee.

THE ORIGINAL CARTER FAMILY    MAYBELLE,   SARA,   A.P. CARTER

Franklin was the first name proposed for the new territory, after statesman Benjamin Franklin, and the state's first governor was John Sevier, who served with Secretary of State Landon Carter. The name Carter would become legendary in East Tennessee music with the likes of A.P. Carter and family, including June Carter Cash. (AOA.)

A.P. Carter and family became the "First Family of Country Music." The Carter Family Fold continues to host weekly performances in Hiltons, Virginia. The site and the weekly performances honor the memory of the legendary A.P., Sara, and Maybelle Carter, whose first recordings, created in 1927, are credited with giving birth to the commercial country music industry. (AOA.)

# Two

# Wexford Girl Becomes the Knoxville Girl

The following lyrics are from the ballad "The Knoxville Girl": "I fell in love with a Knoxville girl, / Her name was Flora Dean. / Her rosy cheeks, her curly hair, / I really did admire. / About nine or ten days after that, / Little Flora she was found. / A floating down by her father's house / Who lived in Knoxville town." (LOC.)

# Cecil J. Sharp and Maud Karpeles
# Eighty English Folk Songs

Specimen piano accompaniments by
**BENJAMIN BRITTEN**

Chord symbols for guitarists by Pat Shaw

So begins and ends the most important of all murder ballads carried across from England to the Appalachians by street singers. Other murder ballads include "Little Sadie," "Banks of the Ohio," and "Pretty Polly." A large number of pieces of ballad journalism have used "The Knoxville Girl" as a song template during the last two and a half centuries. The original comes from a ballad from the end of the 17th century called "The Wittam Miller" (Wittam is a village near Oxford). Most of the 19th-century publishers of ballads printed a version of this favorite, which was the parent ballad of "The Wexford Girl," which became the American murder ballad "The Knoxville Girl." (EFD.)

Ballads and songs became a way to convey the stories, myths, and beliefs of people who were unable to read or write. Ballad journalism captured the images and stories that were important to people from generation to generation. The mountain schools that were an important part of the outreach into Appalachia were founded to teach literacy to an isolated population. (LOC.)

The story of the music of East Tennessee goes back centuries to the fiddle music and ballads of Ireland and the migration of the Scotch-Irish to the Appalachian region of the eastern part of the state. Ultimately, the musical style and genre called bluegrass came from contributors as far south as Florida, as far north as Washington, DC, as far west as western Kentucky, and, most significantly, as far east as Ireland, Scotland, England, and Wales. (LOC.)

The Scotch-Irish who settled in the area largely came from the counties of Northern Ireland—Antrim, Down, Tyrone, Londonderry—and from Donegal, one of the Ulster counties in the Republic of Ireland. Throughout the 18th century, these people immigrated to America in large numbers. They were sturdy, independent people with an appetite to work and were, for the most part, Presbyterians. As they poured into the new country of the United States, they brought their language, accent, instruments, religion, songs, and music. (LOC.)

By the end of the 18th century, the Scotch-Irish had become the most influential segment of the population in the United States next to the English. A large percentage of these immigrants settled in the Appalachian states of North Carolina, Virginia, Kentucky, and Tennessee. (KF.)

The curious aspect of the Scotch-Irish movement into Appalachia and the upland southern states is that they were not recognized as an ethnic or nationalistic group, which is notable because their arrival in Tennessee and Kentucky was the result of a second migration. The first movement came from Ireland, and the second movement from North Carolina and Virginia. By the time they settled farther west and across the mountains in Tennessee and Kentucky, they had already assimilated into the new land and its customs. As they pioneered the new state of Tennessee, they increasingly did so as Americans, not Irish or Scotch settlers. (KF.)

Although the Scotch-Irish quickly merged into the United States, the Ulster speech stayed alive in the hill country of Appalachia. Among the earliest songs were ballads of King William of Orange, and the hill musicians who sang them became known as Billy-boys of the hill country, or, more simply, "hillbillies." The fiddle had become an instrument of major significance in the development of these songs and the one most identified with hillbilly music. (LOC.)

Music accompanied Appalachian culture, but even more permeating were vocabulary and grammar, which were, of course, used by everyone. In his comprehensive study of vocabulary and language migration from Scotch-Irish Ireland to Southern Appalachia, Michael Montgomery identifies grammatical patterns found almost exclusively in East Tennessee and Appalachia. He traces these expressions and grammatical patterns directly to the Scotch-Irish of Northern Ireland. (KF.)

Michael Montgomery states: "East Tennesseeans owe much of their traditional speech to Scotch-Irish emigrants of more than two hundred years ago." Montgomery cites the example of the term "you'uns," a contraction for the joined words "you" and "ones." In East Tennessee, the terms "young'uns" for "young ones" and "big'uns" for "big ones" are still in use. Another example is the combination of the verbs "might" and "could," as in the expression, "I wonder if you might could help me?" Another is the use of the preposition "till" for "to," as in, "It is a quarter till five." (CPM.)

In the novel *River of Earth*, James Still (1906–2001), the first poet laureate of Kentucky, vividly captures Appalachian Mountain speech and the residents' primitive way of life. Still demonstrates these words, expressions, and phrases capturing the rich and archaic poetry of the mountain folk in their talk and customs. (CPM.)

Hearing expressions such as those on the previous page, many outside the region think of this as hillbilly or folk language, calling the terms "hillbilly," "country," "incorrect," "uneducated," "illiterate," or "improper." In fact, these terms are directly related to Scotch-Irish vocabulary and grammar and direct descendants of the speech of East Tennessee. I grew up using these terms and still use them today. They are traditional spoken usage and indicators of a literary style from a bygone day and a former country. (LOC.)

Michael Montgomery argues that the words "pin" and "pen" and "tin" and "ten," which are indistinguishable from each other in East Tennessee pronunciation, can also be traced back to Ulster, Ireland. His study of emigrant letter-writing from the period demonstrates that the interchanging use of the vowels *i* and *e* can be found in the spelling of "gineral" for "general" or "sind" for "send." He connects this interchange as an explanation of what is commonly called the "southern drawl," or what sounds like the addition of an "uh" syllable to a single-syllable word, making "send" into "si-uhnd." (LOC.)

....384 F. Gone Over the Big Divide.

In the motion picture *Songcatcher* (2000), a vivid, if fictionalized, portrayal of life in Appalachia at the beginning of the 20th century, in the many performances of mountain ballads, one can hear how the rhyming scheme of the poetry follows archaic pronunciations of some words, including exact rhymes rather than what would appear in print to be assonance (such as "pen" rhyming with "win"), as well as natural diphthongs that are intentionally a part of the rhyming scheme of the ballad being sung (for example, "kin" rhyming with "send," or "ki-un" and "si-uhnd"). (LOC.)

According to Michael Montgomery, the following words, unique to East Tennessee, have a direct connection to Scotch-Irish vocabulary: airish (chilly), backset (setback), beal (festering boil), bonnyclabber (sour milk), bottomland (low, fertile land), chancy (doubtful, dangerous), contrary (oppose), creel (twist), discomfit (inconvenience), fireboard (mantelpiece), hull (to shell), ill (bad-tempered), kindling (scraps of firewood), let on (pretend), mend (improve), muley (hornless cow), nicker (whinny), palings (fence stakes), piece (a distance), redd up (tidy up), soon (early), and take up (begin). The presence of these words in the lyrics of a song or ballad offer a direct connection to the form's Scotch-Irish origins. (LOC.)

One item of cultural transferral that does not stem from the Ulster Irish is the names of towns throughout East Tennessee. In New England and the upper Atlantic states, it is common to see places named after the European towns from which a majority of the settlers came. This is not the case in East Tennessee due to the fact that the settlers were a generation removed from immigration, so towns had already been named. It is much more likely to find Cherokee or other indigenous derivation for names such as Tellico, Nantahala, and Cherohala, or colonial names such as Sevierville, Knoxville, Knox County (named after Henry Knox), and Clinton (named after Vice President George Clinton). (PO.)

The consensus on Scotch-Irish immigration to America is that at least 150,000 came to the area in the six decades before the Revolutionary War, they were overwhelmingly Presbyterian, the great majority were of Scottish ancestry, and they had left Ireland for economic reasons. (LOC.)

The terrain of East Tennessee bears some resemblance to noncoastal areas of Ireland and Scotland. The mountains have a distinct similarity, but so do the forests, lakes, and foliage. As one moves west across the state, mountains mellow to hills, and farther west, hills disappear into the Mississippi delta. The length of Ireland is 302 miles from north to south and 171 miles from east to west. The horizontal length of Tennessee is 440 miles from east to west. (EFD.)

In 1792, William Blount, a Revolutionary War hero, was appointed by Pres. George Washington as governor of the new territory of East Tennessee and superintendent of Indian affairs in the south. Blount chose the area known as White's Fort as the new capital of the territory, and he commissioned its founder, Gen. James White, to lay out the streets of the town. It was renamed Knoxville after Gen. Henry Knox, Washington's secretary of war, and the surrounding county was also named Knox in tribute, although the general never visited Tennessee. (LOC.)

In January 1796, a general assembly was called in Knoxville to draw up a state constitution. As a result, the US government accepted Tennessee as the 16th state of the Union. (LOC.)

# Three

# READ THE BIBLE, PRAY, GIVE THANKS, AND PLAY FIDDLE

In A.W. Putnam's *History of Middle Tennessee; Or, Life and Times of Gen. James Roberston*, the author gives an account of James Gamble, possibly Tennessee's first professional musician. The account states that "he read his Bible, and fiddled; he prayed, and he fiddled; asked a silent blessing on his meals, gave thanks, and fiddled; went to meetings, sang the songs of Zion, joined in all the devotional services, went home, and fiddled. He sometimes fiddled in bed, but always fiddled when he got up." (PSB.)

The Appalachian Mountains run parallel with the Eastern Seaboard of the United States about 250 miles inland from the Atlantic Ocean. The Appalachian mountain ranges are the Great Smokies, Black Mountains, Blue Ridge Mountains, and the Cumberland Mountains. At the turn of the 20th century, the roads into and out of these mountains were often no more than tracks over the mountains or alongside the riverbeds. Many roads of that time were essentially the actual bed of a river itself. (LOC.)

The mountains form a natural barrier for things coming in to and going out of the East Tennessee region, such as people and supplies, but also fiddle tunes, stories, and ballads. As a result, traditions became lodged and perpetuated in the mountain areas where people settled, creating a fix-and-mend society rather than a consumer or replacement pattern for the region. This was also true for style, music, and culture—the Appalachian mountain region remained relatively unaffected by popular music or new performance customs prior to commercialization and broadcasting in the 1920s. People passed things along from generation to generation, holding on to ballads, fiddle tunes, and stories and images from the past. (EFD.)

A ballad is a poem or song that tells a story in multiple stanzas set to the same tune. This is the structure and form that country and bluegrass songs would also assume. Ballads from the Appalachians are almost always of unknown authorship and were passed along orally from family to family and generation to generation as part of the folk culture and means to preserve history and valued images. Ballads were sung by amateurs for their friends and families' pleasure and entertainment. They usually contain many verses, allowing the entertainment to go on as long as possible. Ballad singers often add, subtract, or alter verses as they please, lending the song timely and local relevance or simply allowing the singer latitude for self-expression. As a result, a classic ballad such as "The Wexford Girl" morphed into "The Knoxville Girl" in East Tennessee. (LOC.)

In his book *An Introduction to Folk Music in the United States*, musicologist Bruno Nettl estimated that there were some 200 British broadside ballads in circulation in the United States, and that "a considerable number, perhaps as many as a third . . . are of Irish origin." A broadside, or broadsheet, is a single sheet of inexpensive paper printed on one side with a ballad, rhyme, news, and sometimes woodcut illustrations. Broadsides were one of the most common forms of printed material between the 16th and 19th centuries, particularly in Britain, Ireland, and North America, and are often associated with one of the most important forms of traditional music from these countries: the ballad. (LOC.)

Many of the mountain ballads originated in the British Isles. These traditional songs were first compiled throughout Appalachia as a result of the work of Frances James Child, who created an inventory of English and Scottish ballads that he had discovered at the end of the 19th century. (LOC.)

Olive Dame Campbell (1882–1954) of Asheville, North Carolina, was the wife of John Campbell, an employee of the Russell Sage Foundation who was engaged in a social project upgrading the Appalachian school system. His job necessitated long trips into the mountains, and Olive often accompanied her husband on his journeys. It was during such trips that she first heard mountain ballads and songs and began to write them down. (EFD.)

Olive Dame Campbell became the founder of the John C. Campbell Folk School and was known as a ballad collector, or songcatcher. On her missions with her husband, John, throughout Appalachia to survey social and economic realities in mountain communities in the early 1900s, she recorded early folk songs and ballads perpetuated from the inhabitants' migration from Ireland, Scotland, Wales, and England. She also corresponded with Cecil J. Sharp (pictured). (EFD.)

In a letter from Olive Dame Campbell to Cecil Sharp on December 20, 1916, the intent of Campbell's efforts is revealed; in her words, it was "the recognition and preservation of all that is native and fine." The Campbells embarked on a lifetime of collaboration in Appalachian social projects, beginning with the trips they took in the fall of 1908 and the spring of 1909 in southern Appalachia through eastern Kentucky, eastern Tennessee, western North Carolina, and parts of West Virginia and northern Georgia. This effort resulted in Campbell inviting Sharp to come to Appalachia to collect songs captured within the confines of the Appalachian mountains. Sharp (left) and his assistant Maud Karpeles, both seated, are pictured here. (EFD.)

# 19 BARBARA ELLEN

O down in Lon - don where I was raised, Down where I got my learn-ing ___ I ___ fell in love with a pret-ty lit-tle girl. Her name was ___ Bar - b'ry ___ El-len.

In December 1907, Olive Dame and John Campbell visited Hindman Settlement School in Kentucky, and it was there that Olive heard a student, Ada Smith, sing a version of the ballad "Barbara Allen." Olive wrote about this encounter in her journal/diary: "Shall I ever forget it. The blazing fire, the young girl on her low stool before it, the soft strange strumming of the banjo—different from anything I had heard before—and then the song. I had been used to singing 'Barbara Allen' as a child, but how far from that gentle tune was this—so strange, so remote, so thrilling."

At the invitation of Olive Dame Campbell, Cecil J. Sharp (1859–1924), music teacher and ethnomusicologist from south London, came to Appalachia with his assistant Maud Karpeles (1885–1976) to record the Irish, Scottish, and English folk songs and ballads that were still being performed in the most remote areas of East Tennessee and Appalachia. Sharp was England's most renowned collector of folk music and dances, noting and documenting nearly 5,000 tunes in his travels throughout England and the Appalachian states up until his death in 1924. His vast Appalachian collection was assembled during the First World War period in North Carolina, Virginia, West Virginia, Kentucky, and Tennessee. Sharp and Karpeles embarked on a remarkable journey to discover a living tradition of songs and ballads, largely of British origin, that had all but died out in England. From 1916 to 1918, they collected over 1,600 songs and variants during their travels throughout Appalachia. (LOC.)

The following description is from Cecil Sharp's diary entry on July 26, 1916, upon his arrival in Knoxville and the start of his Appalachian journey: "Maud [Karpeles] and I left New York in tropical heat on Sunday afternoon, got to Knoxville on Monday at 1.30, left for Copper Hill an hour or so later, arriving at this very primitive little mining village at 10 P.M. Our train left at 6.30 A.M. yesterday (Tuesday), got on to Murphy at 11, where we changed onto the Southern Railway, and eventually arrived here at 11.30 P.M.—or, rather, what was left of us." (EFD.)

Eighteen days later, on August 13, 1916, these are Sharp's initial analysis: "I am still in the mountains. The journey on the day after I last wrote to you was indescribably terrible. I should not have believed wheels and horses could get over such tracks unless I had seen the thing done. I was frightened out of my life. Now Maud and I walk about everywhere, except occasionally we have to take a jolt-wagon (well named!). The country is, I think, the most magnificent I have ever seen. The mountains are everywhere, and we live in the valleys and walk through the passes. The mountains go from six thousand feet, and the valleys two or a little over. The weather has been very hot indeed, and I go about in a shirt and pair of flannel trousers, and keep as cool as I can. My experiences have been very wonderful so far as the people and their music is concerned. The people are just English of the late eighteenth or early nineteenth century. They speak English, look English, and their manners are old-fashioned English. Heaps of words and expressions they use habitually in ordinary conversation are obsolete, and have been in England a long time. I find them very easy to get on with, and have no difficulty in making them sing and show their enthusiasm for their songs. I have taken down very nearly one hundred already, and many of these are quite unknown to me and aesthetically of the very highest value. Indeed, it is the greatest discovery I have made since the original one I made in England sixteen years ago. This last week I spent three whole days, from 10 A.M. to 5.30 P.M., with a family in the mountains consisting of parents and daughter, by name Hensley. All three sang and the father played the fiddle. Maud and I dined with them each day, and the rest of the time sat on the veranda while the three sang and played and talked, mainly about the songs. I must have taken down thirty tunes from them and have not yet exhausted them. One ballad, 'The Cruel Mother,' is by far the finest variant, both words and tune, which, in my opinion, has yet been found." (LOC.)

Maud Karpeles, Cecil Sharp's assistant, describes her experience in Appalachia in 1916–1918: "The people lived in primitive log-cabins dotted along the banks of the rivers, or creeks as they were called. They were nearly self-supporting, building their own log-cabins, spinning and weaving the wool for their clothes and growing their own food. Their living was not luxurious, but they had leisure and that they prized more than material comfort and possessions." (LOC.)

Cecil Sharp wrote the influential volume *English Folk Song: Some Conclusions*. In his writing, he describes a category of "lonesome and love tunes" found in Appalachian songs and ballads. These are often mournful ballads that dealt with loss of life and love—a recurring theme in many early bluegrass songs. The compilation he published with Olive Dame Campbell, *English Folk Songs from the Southern Appalachians* (1917) is an extensive collection of songs from West Virginia, western Virginia, western North Carolina, East Tennessee, the northwest tip of South Carolina, northern Georgia, and northern Alabama.

The following is from Cecil Sharp's diary entry written on Friday, September 1, 1916, in Rocky Fork, Tennessee, a Smoky Mountain town 50 miles from Bristol, Tennessee: "Mrs. Crane having arranged to take us to see her father Mr. Blankenship we left home at 7 and called for her. She took us a weary stony walk up to the top of Higgins Creek where we made friends with the B[lankenship] family a large number of relatives belonging to three or more generations! Got a few songs and on the way home called on Mr. and Mrs. Coates (Flag Pond, TN) from the latter of whom I got a fine ballad 'The False Knight [on the Road]' and an interesting variant of 'Wraggle Taggle Gipsies O.' Altogether a very successful if fatiguing day. We must have walked 14 miles over very bad tracks. We got back thoroughly tired out at 6.30 p.m. nearly 12 hours since we left in the morning." The ballad "The False Knight upon the Road" was published in Cecil Sharp's 1918 collection *American-English Folk-Ballads from the Southern Appalachian Mountains* (Set 22). The piano accompaniment was written by Sharp.

In Maud Karpeles's unpublished autobiography, she has this to say about "The False Knight in the Road": "But I think that the greatest prize was the one that we secured at the end of a long and disappointing day when we had been on the go from six a.m. to six p.m. We had obtained practically nothing of value, and when we were within a few miles of the end of our tramp we noticed a log-cabin perched on top of a sharp incline. We debated whether we should or should not make one more attempt and finally decided to call at the cabin, though not very hopefully; but after a short conversation there fell on our ears 'The False Knight in the Road', surely one of the most dramatic ballads in the English language." (LOC.)

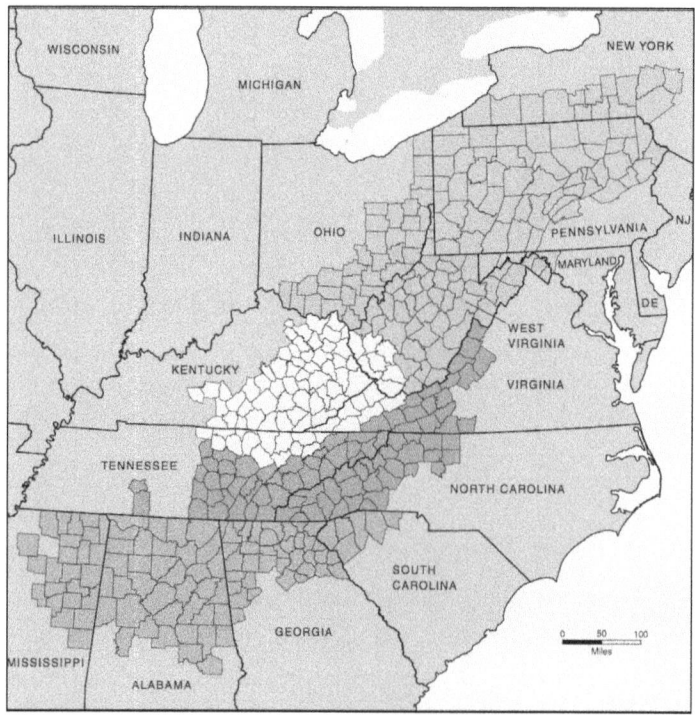

Whether it is an early contribution by an unknown author or a contemporary tune such as "I Will Always Love You," written and recorded by singer/songwriter Dolly Parton, who was born in a one-room cabin on the banks of the Little Pigeon River in Sevier County in the Smoky Mountains of East Tennessee, ballad themes have remained much the same. (LOC.)

Tracing the collective travels of Olive Dame Campbell, Maud Karpeles, and Cecil Sharp throughout Appalachia reveals their intrepid dedication to song collection in some of the most remote areas. It also marks the beginning of the awareness of this musical heritage in the region and throughout the world that eventually led to the recording of this music and its professionalization, development, commercial performance, distribution, and mass broadcast. The highlighted areas on this map represent the counties of Appalachia.

*Four*

# THE LONESOME VALLEY

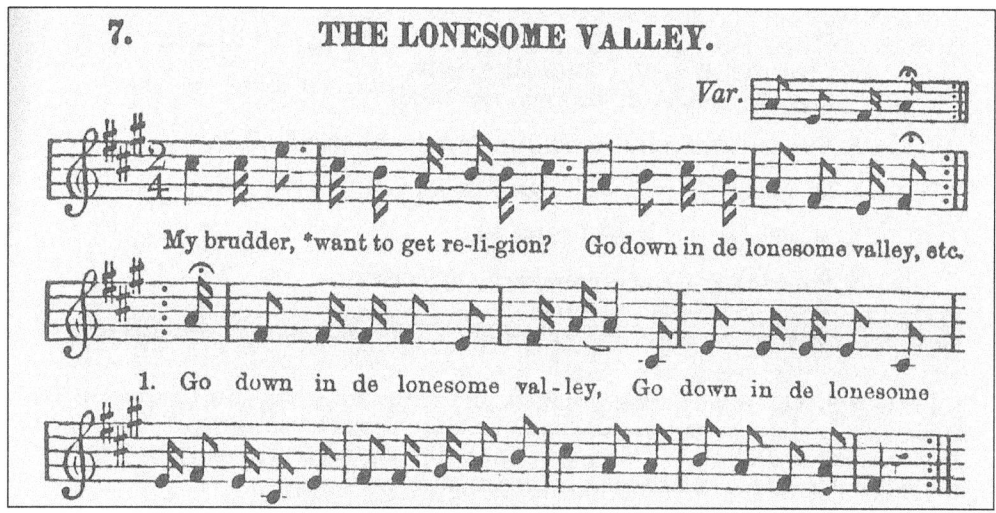

Noted ethnomusicologist George Pullen Jackson (1874–1953) collected and studied Appalachian folk songs and spirituals and, like Cecil J. Sharp, noted a category of ballads and spirituals using the word "lonesome." In particular, the spiritual title "Lonesome Valley" may have come from the song "In Seaport Town," one of the songs collected by Cecil Sharp in 1916, which uses this recurring phrase: "They wandered over the hills and mountains / And through a many of a place unknown, / 'Till at last they came to a lonesome valley / And there they killed him dead alone."

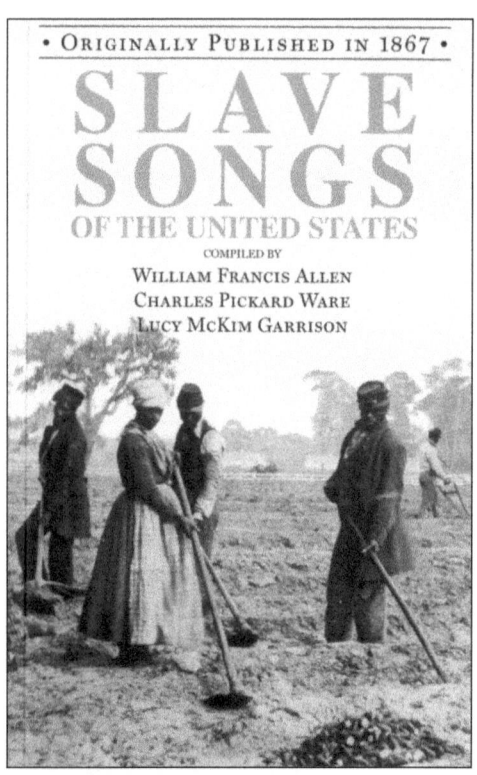

The important 1867 collection of spirituals of the southern United States, *Slave Songs of the United States*, compiled by William Frances Allen, Charles Pickard Ware, and Lucy McKim Garrison, contains the song "The Lonesome Valley" (No. 7). Variations on this spiritual exist in versions such as this: "Jesus walked this lonesome valley; / He had to walk it by himself; / Oh, nobody else could walk it for him; / He had to walk it by himself." "Lonesome Valley" is important to the story of bluegrass due to the words "lonesome," "valley," and "walk." "Lonesome" would be used to characterize the bluegrass sound of Bill Monroe, the "Father of Bluegrass," and his band the Blue Grass Boys, as coined by the phrase "high lonesome sound." "Valley" has theological implications as well as geographical realities for Appalachian life, representing Biblical days in the wilderness as well as "mountain people." And "walk it" was a transportation reality due to the remoteness of the Appalachian terrain. Prior to modern roads, there simply was no way to travel from point to point in certain areas other than on foot or horseback.

This image shows the author's grandfather Hobert Estep (the man farthest to the left) supervising one of many Works Progress Administration (WPA) bridge projects created between 1935 and 1943 to span the valleys and connect the mountains throughout Appalachia.

English ethnomusicologist Cecil Sharp used these words to describe the geography of Appalachian eastern Tennessee after his tour of the area: "The region is from its inaccessibility a very secluded one. There are but few roads—most of them little better than mountain tracks—and practically no railroads. Indeed, so remote and shut off from outside influence were, until quite recently, these sequestered mountain valleys that the inhabitants have for a hundred years or more been completely isolated and cut off from all traffic with the rest of the world." This description further underscores the significance of the word "lonesome" as a recurring theme in songs from Appalachia, including combinations such as "lonesome night," "lonesome grave," "lonesome day," "lonesome dove," and "lonesome valley." "Lonesome Valley" appears to be the most prominent in the list of lonesome songs and is certainly iconic in the remote Appalachian experience. (Above, LOC.)

"Lonesome" songs such as "Do, Lord, Remember Me," and various songs written or sung by Ralph and Carter Stanley feature a melancholy and often fatalistic message and tone in which the characters portrayed in the narrative are caught in events over which they have no control or must live with the consequences of their actions. (LOC.)

Stanley Bros. looking into three states at historic Cumberland Gap

### LITTLE GLASS OF WINE

Come little girl, let's go get married,
I love you so great, how can you slight me;
I'll work for you both late and early,
At my wedding my little wife you'll be.

Oh Willie dear, let's both consider,
We're both too young to be married now;
When we're married, we're bound together,
Let's stay single just one more year.

He went to the ball where she was dancing,
A jealous thought came through his mind;
I'll kill that girl, my own true lover,
Before I'll let another man beat my time.

He went to the bar and he called her to him,
She said, Willie dear, what do you want with me,
Come and drink wine with the one that loves you,
More than anyone else in the world, said he.

While they were at the bar a-drinking,
That same old thought came through his mind;
He killed that girl, his own true lover,
He gave her poison in a glass of wine.

She laid her head over on his shoulder,
Said, Willie dear, please take me home,
That glass of wine that I've just dranken
Has gone to my head and got me wrong.

He laid his head over on the pillow,
Let me read you the law, let me tell you my mind;
Molly dear, I'm sorry to tell you
We both drank poison in a glass of wine.

They fold their arms around each other,
They cast their eyes into the sky;
Oh God, Oh God, ain't this a pity,
That we both true lovers are bound to die.

In "White Dove," written by Ralph Stanley's brother Carter, we hear these melancholy words: "White dove will mourn and sorrow, / The willows hang their head. / I'll live my life in sorrow / Since Mother and Daddy are dead." (AOA.)

On September 14, 1916, Cecil Sharp recorded the words collected in the final verse of the mountain ballad "Good Morning My Pretty Little Miss": "I can sing as lonesome a song / As any little bird in the cage. / O sixteen weeks astray have been gone / And scarcely fifteen years of age." He also recorded these words from the ballad "Awake! Awake!": "I'll go down in some lone valley, / I'll spend my weeks, my months, my years. / And I'll eat nothing but green willow / And I'll drink nothing but my tears." (FDS.)

Another Tennessee ballad specifically referenced the wilderness as a spiritual destination: "I sought my Lord in de wilderness, / For I'm a-going home. / I found free grace in the wilderness . . . / My father preaches in the wilderness." Yet another contains lyrics with a wilderness invitation: "Way down in de valley, / Who will rise and go with me? / You've heern talk of Jesus, / Who set poor sinners free."

59

"Valley" and "lonesome valley" were familiar words in the wilderness religious experience. To descend into that region implied the same process as that of the camp meeting's "anxious seat," which was reserved for a person concerned about their spiritual condition in hopes that the afflicted soul might experience a religious conversion. Other songs that mention "lonesome" and "lonesome valley" position this recurring phrase in a specific emotional environment. (LOC.)

# 39 PRETTY SARO

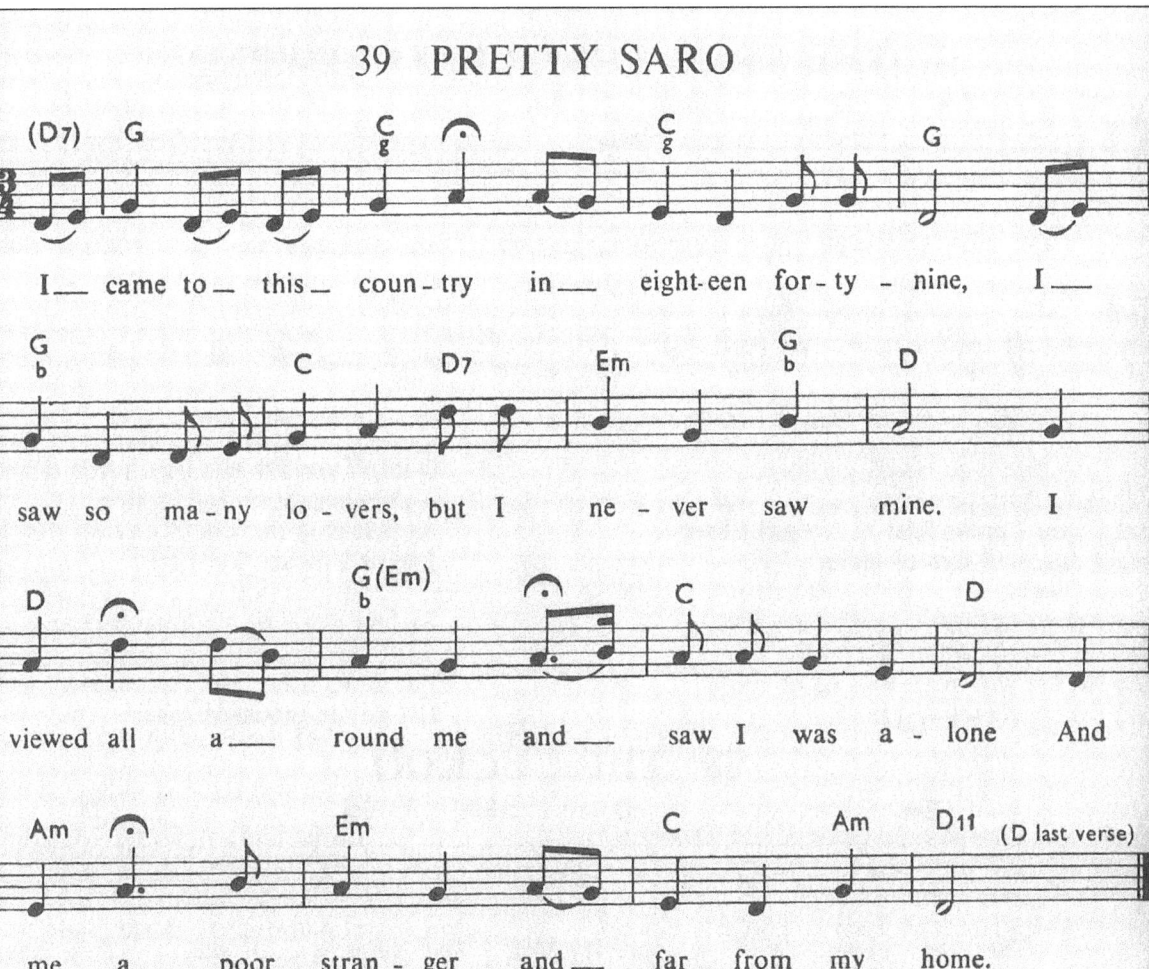

"Pretty Saro," another ballad collected by Sharp and Karpeles, speaks to unrequited love: "Down in some lonesome valley, down in some lone place, / Where the small birds do whistle their notes to increase; / But when I get sorrow, I'll set down and cry / And think of my darling, my darling so nigh." In "Young Hunting," Lady Margaret murders loving Henry with a knife when he refuses her advances: "Who cares I for your bow and arrow, / And it all in its prime, / I fly away to some lonesome valley / And 'light on some high pine." "The Sweet Primroses" is the story of a young lady in need of comfort who rejects the advances of a deceitful young man and admonishes him: "I will take thee down to some lonesome valley, / Where no man nor mortal shall ever me tell; / Where the pretty little small birds do change their voices, / And every moment their notes do swell."

The remote geography of the Appalachian Mountains would bring the "lonesome" theme to the music and stories that morphed into the genre known as bluegrass in the 1940s and characterize the sounds of these transported ballads and the music of the new storytellers of this emerging art form. But things were destined for change in Appalachia. In the book *Miners, Millhands, and Mountaineers*, Ronald D. Eller writes about the emerging Appalachia: "What had been in 1860 only the quiet backcountry of the Old South became by the turn of the century a new frontier for expanding industrial capitalism." (LOC.)

# Five
# CULTURES COLLIDE, CREATING A NEW ART FORM

Bluegrass music is a relatively recent addition to the family of country music subgenres that originated from the same grouping of acoustic string-band instruments associated with classic country but with features that merit it having its own category and allow it to stand alone. (AOA.)

Bluegrass music stems from the mountain ballads and fiddling traditions found throughout Southern Appalachia. Variations on preexisting song themes were created as new influences and cultures of traditional musical material converged in the Appalachian mountain areas. New combinations took shape as the Irish fiddle, the African/Caribbean banjo, the Italian mandolin, and the European guitar and string bass met in fresh and exciting ensembles and an explosive clash of cultures. (LOC.)

New arrivals brought their values, stories, and songs—along with their attitudes, lingering feuds, and political arguments—to the New World. This cultural baggage, along with human confrontation, informed and influenced early settlements in every way. Geographical barriers kept some of this development in check for a while, but over time, population patterns, industrialization, and the need for work ultimately led to a convergence of various cultures with native as well as diverse immigrant influences.

British folk-song collector Cecil J. Sharp observed one consistency throughout the developing culture and patterns of the early settlers, which he described as "the true, sincere, ideal expression of human feeling and imagination." Music from all of the gathering cultures had this expression in common. Early settlers carried with them the need to sing and express their feelings of hope, despair, loneliness, love, and their Old World memories and New World aspirations. (LOC.)

The thousands of songs and ballads that circulated throughout Appalachia and that flooded into the valleys of the Cumberland and Tennessee Rivers came from the lips of generations of folk performers. Song, story, and dance culture was bequeathed to early settlers from their ancestors from Ireland, Scotland, Wales, and England. "Pretty Saro" is a ballad that tells this story: "I came to this country in eighteen forty nine, / I saw so many lovers, but I never saw mine. / I viewed all around me and saw I was alone / And me a poor stranger and far from my home." (KF.)

**RALPH STANLEY**

In the prologue to his life story *Man of Constant Sorrow: My Life and Times*, Bluegrass musician and Virginia Appalachia native Ralph Stanley describes isolation in his own life: "This was a long time ago, back in the 1930s, and a long way back in steep hills and deep hollows. Where I come from, people lived spread out from one another. There was no radio or telephone. Days would pass between you seeing anybody outside your family. Singing was a way to keep yourself company when you got to feeling lonesome." (AOA.)

Stanley continued, "Songs were handed down from father to son and mother to daughter." But by the 1920s, commercial recording was coming of age, and there was a growing appetite among broadcast media and recording companies for the unique sounds coming out of the hill country from string bands and "Old Time" music groups. These string bands, family bands, mountain music, hillbilly music, and, ultimately, country music that would lead to bluegrass were part of this wave. (LOC.)

Transposed to America, the fiddle reached the peak of its development in Southern Appalachia. In the latter half of the 1880s, the fiddle-banjo duet arrived, and in the early 1900s, fiddle, banjo, and guitar trios were being formed in the southern mountains. Mountain musicians proudly displayed their instruments in their portraits and photographs from the era. (CPM.)

For country music and bluegrass, the solidification of the beginning of this genre and subgenre came with the broadcasting of the music as a result of the recording industry. In 1922, Victor Talking Machine Company recorded what would be hailed as the first country, or hillbilly, record. Accomplished fiddler Alexander Campbell Robertson, known as Eck, traveled to New York City with Henry C. Gililand to record for RCA Victor. Their first song was "Arkinsaw Traveler," followed by "Apple Blossom," "Forked Deer," and "Turkey in the Straw." (LOC.)

Ernest Stoneman went to New York and recorded country music, and Stoneman helped line up musicians in the Appalachian south for the historic Bristol, Tennessee, recording sessions. "Pop" Stoneman sold a lot of recordings himself and also had 23 children, all of whom played and sang in various versions of his own family band at some point.

What is now cleverly called the "Big Bang" of country music occurred when Ralph Peer, director of the OKeh Record Company (its name was derived from the initials of founder Otto K.E. Heinemann), established a makeshift recording studio in Bristol, Tennessee, the bifurcated city in Tennessee and Virginia with the state line running right through the middle of town. This occurred over a two-week period in the summer of 1927, when Peer advertised a wide invitation for musicians of the region to audition, with the prize being a recording contract. Mountain musicians came from as far as Bluefield, West Virginia, to record on 78-rpm vinyl for those audition sessions. (LOC.)

The Bristol recordings varied from Scotch-Irish fiddle tunes and ballads to gospel hymns and blues songs. During this flash of convergence, the two most important acts in early country music were discovered: the Carter Family and Jimmie Rodgers. (LOC.)

Thanks to the Bristol recording sessions, in one fell swoop, Ralph Peer snatched up mountain musical acts of all descriptions, freezing a moment in time as he created recordings destined for radio play and mass dissemination. The region's multiracial and intersecting traditions would truly bring into being the genre known as country music, from which bluegrass would emerge a few years later. (LOC.)

Regional traditions were embodied in the talents of Clinch Mountain musicians A.P. Carter and his wife, Sara, and sister-in-law Maybelle and Mississippi yodeler Jimmie Rodgers, who, in 1927, was based around Asheville, North Carolina. Rodgers would go on to be hailed as "the Father of Country Music" and one of the first recording stars in the country. To this writer's ears, many of the traits of later bluegrass music can be heard in the recordings of Jimmie Rodgers. The Carter Family, from western Virginia, would go on to earn the title "the First Family of Country Music." (AOA.)

From these beginnings, an entire genre of music blossomed out of Bristol in East Tennessee. This genre is universally celebrated as country music, but many music critics would define this early aggregation as a genre in itself, separate from country—Appalachian music. The songs were drawn from a melting pot of gospel songs, shape-note hymns, ballads from the old country, folk ballads, minstrel songs, early blues songs, and parlor songs such as "Wildwood Flower," which, although it may sound ancient, was actually written by professional songwriter J.P. Webster, from New Hampshire, in 1860. (AOA.)

The intersection of this body of talent, the ability to capture performances on recordings, and the exponential growth of new broadcasting empires hungry for new material all converged in a perfect storm for the birth of the genre that would be called country. The fuel for this launch came from Appalachia but was ignited in Bristol and East Tennessee. (AOA.)

Jimmie Rodgers had teamed up with the Tenneva Ramblers from Bristol when the band heard that Ralph Peer and his Victor Talking Machine Company were coming to Bristol to record area musicians. Rodgers and the group arrived in Bristol on August 3, 1927, and auditioned for Peer, who agreed to record them the next day. According to Rodgers's biography, that night, the band argued about how it would be billed on the record, which led Jimmie to declare, "All right, I'll just sing one myself." (AOA.)

The year 1927 was a very optimistic time for the nation in general and would prove to be the launching point for country music. In 1927, Charles Lindbergh completed the first transatlantic flight; *The Jazz Singer* opened in theaters, ending the age of the silent film; the Ford Motor Company began production of their Model A automobile; carving work began on Mount Rushmore; and country music was born in Bristol, Tennessee. Ominously, two years later, the stock market would crash, instigating the Great Depression. (LOC.)

# Six
# THE GRASS IS BLUER ON THE OTHER SIDE

Bluegrass is a unique term among the range of musical styles and forms. Among other styles, such as rock and roll, romanticism, country, western, minimalism, impressionism, polka, or anything else, no other genre of music is named after a type of vegetation grown in a unique region of the world. (LOC.)

The name of this vegetation comes from the illusion presented by the type of grass that grows in northern Kentucky, a species of grasses of the genus *Poa*. When this grass goes to seed, the leaves are green, but the seeds are blue. When one gazes at a field full of this strand of grass, the impression is indeed of a field of blue rather than the usual green grass. For this reason, the state of Kentucky adopted the nickname "the Bluegrass State." Bill Monroe chose to name his band after his native state, and, ultimately, the genre took its name from his band. Monroe always announced what state his band members were from, and he was always introduced as a boy from Kentucky. (AOA.)

Bluegrass music was not far behind the development of country music, arriving in the early 1940s through the overdrive talent, phenomenal songs, business savvy, and general prowess of Rosine, Kentucky, native Bill Monroe and his band, the Blue Grass Boys. (AOA.)

In the simple and direct words of country music historian Neil Rosenberg, "Bluegrass is part of country music; it originated with Bill Monroe and his band, the Blue Grass Boys, during the 1940s." Although the roots of bluegrass come from the same Appalachian traditions as country music, bluegrass has been a professional and commercial music genre from its very first notes. (AOA.)

In the motion picture *Matewan*, a 1987 film about coal mining and union workers in the southwestern region of West Virginia where the author grew up, one scene in a mountain coal camp depicts the likely unsung and obscure beginnings of this combination of string band instruments. As miners who had come from Ireland, Italy, Africa, and other parts of Europe to find work gathered around a campfire at night, each brought a native instrument in a rare moment of nonwork cultural intermingling. Similar to the origins of the various miners, their instruments and stories also came from different nations and were melded in their experiences in their new home in Appalachia. (AOA.)

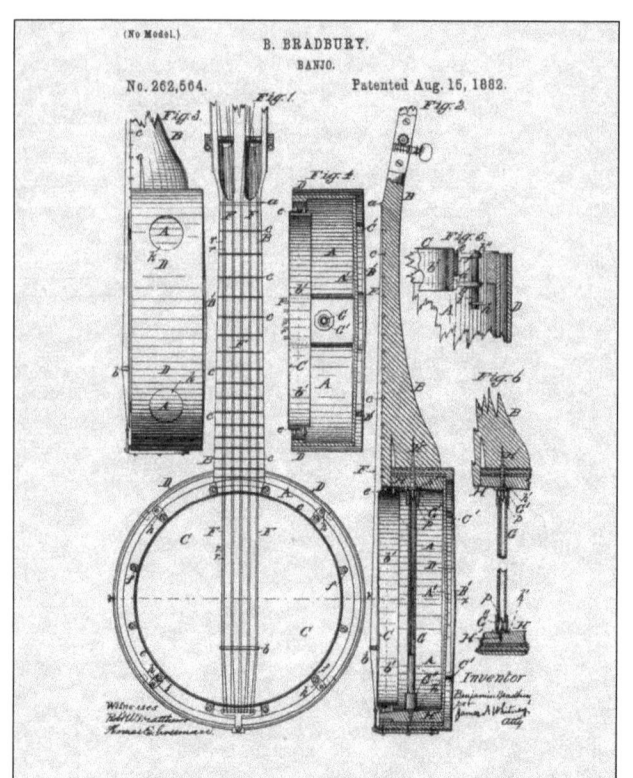

The violin (fiddle), mandolin, double bass, and guitar were no strangers to European immigrants in the United States, but the banjo would become an exotic addition, and its distinctive timbre added to any combination of these instruments threw the bluegrass ensemble into new stylistic territory. Furthermore, the banjo became the musical symbol of Appalachia. Its appearance in the southern states and Appalachia resulted from the influx of African slaves in the mountains.

The banjo as we know it emerged on the North American continent in the 19th century. Modern scholarship demonstrates that it came from Caribbean slaves of West African descent who had made lutes similar to the African akonting, a banjo-shaped instrument made from a hollowed-out gourd covered with an animal hide that features animal-hair strings. (LOC.)

By the 1840s, instrument makers started stretching animal hide over circular bodies made of wood with fretless necks. As the instrument continued to develop, metal bodies, metal strings, and frets were added to the instrument, and even later, amplification was increased by a resonator ring and a solid back. Joel Sweeney, a popular minstrel performer, is credited with adding the fifth string and resonator to the banjo around this time, but there is evidence that a fifth string existed long before Sweeney. There would have been no Earl Scruggs–style banjo picking without these changes to the original form of the instrument.

By the mid-19th century, the banjo had become common in mining and lumber camps and on construction sites of the railways throughout Appalachia. The most famous railroad song to come out of the mountains tells the folk tale of an African American railroad worker in West Virginia in the 1870s, John Henry: "John Henry was about three days old / Sittin' on his papa's knee / He picked up a hammer and a little piece of steel; / Said, 'Hammer's gonna be the death of me, Lord, Lord / Hammer's gonna be the death of me.' / The captain said to John Henry / 'Gonna bring that steam drill 'round / Gonna bring that steam drill out on the job / Gonna whop that steel on down, down, down.'" (LOC.)

By the early 20th century, the five-string banjo had been fitted with an elaborate fretted neck and became a mainstay of ragtime, jazz, Dixieland, and even orchestral music. (CPM.)

Ingredients for popular songs of the 1850s included a catchy tune, a southern setting, a touch of comedy, overtones of courtship, and a song about the banjo. Minstrel shows and their songs dominated U.S. stages by 1880, and a banjo craze also broke out across the country. (LOC.)

The popularity of the banjo was especially strong among middle-class women in the North, prompting an increase in banjo manufacturing in urban centers. Samantha Bumgarner was a fiddle and banjo player from North Carolina who, in 1924, became the first woman to record mountain music, opening doors for other great female musicians who followed. It was common for women to learn to play banjo, and the early banjo icons often credited a sister or mother for introducing them to the banjo. (LOC.)

Among many losses that resulted from the stock market crash of 1929, the economic shutdown wiped out the popularity of the banjo. In the words of Robert Webb, "Demand for its bright happy sound disappeared almost overnight. Professional orchestras made a quick transition to the 'archtop' guitar, developed in the 1920s by Gibson and others which provided a mellow and integral rhythm more in keeping with the subdued nature of the times." (LOC.)

The dobro was added to bluegrass music when East Tennessee native Josh Graves was hired by Lester Flatt and Earl Scruggs to join their band, the Foggy Mountain Boys. At first, "Uncle Josh" Graves of Tellico Plaines, Tennessee, was to work as bassist and comedian, a common addition to early bands. However, his dobro playing was so well received that Lester and Earl moved him to playing dobro full-time, giving the combo a distinctive modern flare and distancing the band from Bill Monroe and his Blue Grass Boys. Dobro was the brand name of an instrument originally built and sold by the Dopyera Brothers in the 1930s, hence the name "Dobro." It became the default name for all resonator guitars. (AOA.)

Josh Graves started his life as a professional musician at age 15. In his words, "I was born September 27, 1927, in Tellico Plains, in Tennessee. Nothing there but mountains, and that's what I love." He was deeply immersed in the mountain music and styles of Appalachia, learning not only from family and peers but also through the emerging medium of radio and recording. The dobro quickly became an integral part of bluegrass music, and other bands soon began adding this instrument to their ensembles. (LOC.)

By the late 1930s, the United States was emerging from the Great Depression, and the music of the era reflected the growing optimism, with the banjo making a return to popularity. (LOC.)

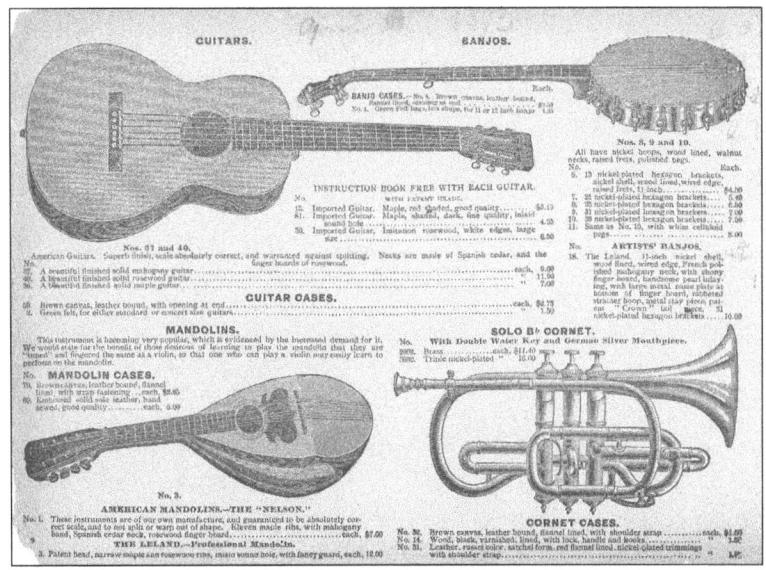

Two playing techniques associated with Appalachian and bluegrass banjo are drones and rolls. Rolls are right-hand fingering patterns that accompany and ornament a melody and consist of eighth notes that subdivide the sounds in each measure. Drone notes are usually eighth notes played on the fifth string to fill in around the melody notes. These techniques, along with fast strumming styles, are idiomatic to the banjo in all styles, and their sound is fundamental to bluegrass. (AOA.)

"The Sabbath among Slaves."

Early in its history, the banjo was played in the clawhammer style, including by Africans who brought the banjo design with them to the United States. Clawhammer-style banjo-playing consists of the downward striking of one or more of the four main strings with the index, middle, or both fingers while the drone or fifth string is played with a lifting (as opposed to downward plucking) motion of the thumb. The notes sounded by the thumb in this fashion are typically played on the offbeat. (LOC.)

The bluegrass band consists first and foremost of fiddle and banjo, then mandolin, guitar, double bass, dobro (occasionally), and lead vocals and harmonies provided by a combination of singers. This distinctive combination of essential instruments is at the core of the bluegrass sound and represents the distinctive combinations that would only be found in Appalachia as a result of converging cultures: Irish fiddle and bass, Italian mandolin, African banjo, and the Spanish guitar.

The accordion almost made it into the bluegrass ensemble but did not make the final cut. The dobro comes in and out of the ensemble but is not a part of what is now considered the "classic" bluegrass sound, despite how forlorn and lonesome the dobro can sound. Flatt and Scruggs most likely used the dobro because of its commercial appeal and unique modern sound, giving their ensemble some competitive edge with the sounds coming from Elvis and rockabilly music. It also helped distance them from an association with the competing Bill Monroe style. There was a distinct rivalry between these ensembles in the early days of bluegrass, and the dobro represented a new development. It may be a coincidence, but Flatt and Scruggs were invited to join the Grand Ole Opry the same year they added dobro. In the ever-emerging "newgrass" subgenre, sounds coming from classical bluegrass, percussion, and other instruments eventually augmented the classic five-instrument configuration.

Though rarely recognized in the same way, another essential part of the band came with modernization in the form of the microphone. The microphone must be considered the "passive" instrument in the composition of the bluegrass ensemble. Since bluegrass is generally played on acoustic instruments, amplification is usually desired in the performance settings. The microphone is a significant 20th-century contribution to the old-time combination of acoustic instruments featured in bluegrass bands. In classic-performance fashion, many bands work a single microphone almost as visual choreography in their live performance routines. (AOA.)

The role of the instruments of the bluegrass band alternates between lead and melodic display and ornamentation, harmonic or rhythmic contrast and accompaniment, and harmonic and rhythmic bass or foundation. Lead parts are most often played by the fiddle, mandolin, banjo, or guitar, while the guitar and double bass provide a harmonic foundation for the sound. (AOA.)

# Seven
# A High Lonesome Sound

Ralph and Bill

Vocals for bluegrass music follow the same pattern as the instrumental layers. A solo voice will provide the lead melody, while a second tenor voice will often provide a high, descant-like drone or duet part to the lead melody. These two voices provide that high lonesome sound that is part of the unique bluegrass signature, incorporating the lonesome theme in a sonic dimension as identified in the ballads of Appalachia. When a third or fourth voice is added, the purpose of the additional voice is to fill in the harmony; it can be above the melody but is most often below the melody note with a bass note sometimes added to fill out the chord. (AOA.)

One Scotch-Irish element of vocal harmony that has remained in bluegrass music is the use of the drone note, most often associated with the sound of the bagpipes. This is the constant single pitch that remains in play while a melody is sung to that single, sustained, and higher-drone pitch. This is heard in vocals and is also characteristic of the single G string (the shortest string) of the five-string banjo. (AOA.)

The evolution of the harmony heard in bluegrass music has a strong resemblance and likely connection to the use of harmony in singing in rural churches across southern Appalachia. Shape-note singing is largely a three- and four-part occurrence and was in wide practice throughout the South following the Second Great Awakening in the early 1800s.

The haunting calls and high-pitched harmonies later dubbed the high lonesome sound came from Bill Monroe and Ralph Stanley's experience with hymn singing in their youth. The singing of Bill Monroe and his Blue Grass Boys offers clear examples of these harmonic techniques, and one can hear this characteristic in the first song Bill Monroe wrote and recorded, "A Voice from on High." (AOA.)

The "high lonesome sound" can be heard in the music of Flatt and Scruggs, the Stanley Brothers, the Del McCoury Band, Jim and Jesse, most every early bluegrass band, and later luminaries such as Ricky Skaggs and Kentucky Thunder and Alison Krauss and Union Station. A case can be made for this sound stretching all the way back to Jimmie Rodgers and his yodeling. (AOA.)

This is Ralph Stanley's account of the vocal approach in his music: "The biggest reason I went back to the a cappella style was simple. It was who I was, as a singer and as a believer, too. I reckon it was the old Primitive Baptist in me. I just grew up singing like that, and I wanted to hear it again. I like to sing the old-time way and I believe in those old-time hymns." (AOA.)

The vocal tendencies of Appalachian folk were eventually labeled hillbilly, country, or backward due to the isolation of those singing and uttering the songs and expressions. Geographical remoteness perpetuated the idea of the "hillbilly" and led to this term being used as a descriptor of many elements of Appalachian life and the inhabitants of the area. (LOC.)

The high range and tessitura (the part of the range where most of the notes reside) of the drone or high tenor note, characterized by high lonesome, is credited as coming from a song entitled "High Lonesome" (recorded in 1958 on the Starday label) by the band Country Gentlemen and later included on Bill Monroe's 1966 album, *The High, Lonesome Sound of Bill Monroe*. This is a rather late-term designation in the progression of the bluegrass genre, but all things considered, bluegrass is not that old of a genre in the first place. That it developed out of fiddle tunes and folk origins gives the impression that it is an ancient musical form, but it is not and actually evolved, in its own way, out of country music. (AOA.)

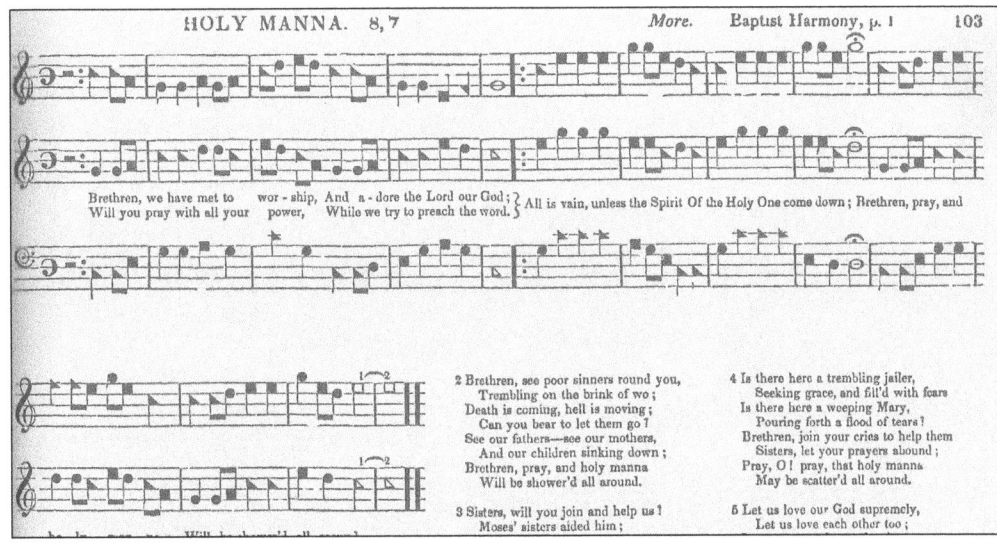

Singing schools were instigated in the 18th century, first in New England by leading musical leaders such as William Billings, in order to teach congregations how to sing new church hymns by writers such as Isaac Watts. These hymns replaced the rhymed and metered psalms that constituted singing practice in churches since the time of the Reformation.

Utilizing a shape-note system of music reading, new hymn settings were taught and spread throughout the south through singing schools led by itinerant experts in the medium. Accompanying these singing schools was the publication of "long boy" hymn, or shape-note, songbooks, so-called due to their wide horizontal shape. Music literacy was provided through these shape-note singing schools.

Singing-school classes sat on long benches in a hollow square, and the teacher stood in the middle of the square. The leader would move about in this middle area, working his way through the various treble, tenor, counter, and bass sections. The treble corresponded to the modern tenor, the tenor corresponded to the soprano, the counter to the alto, and the bass to the bass. Women sang treble. As the leader vigorously kept time with long sweeps of the arms and hands, every singer was required to closely imitate his every movement. His chief accomplishment was the ability to sing any part in the music, and whenever bass, tenor, counter, or treble lagged behind or broke down in the performance, the leader would run to the support of the wavering line and bring up the stragglers. (LOC.)

The first shape-note folk hymn used the four-shape system of notation called fasola and, later, developed to the seven-note system called doremi. The four-shape system first appeared in William Smith and William Little's *The Easy Instructor* (1801) and Andrew Law's *The Musical Primer* (1801), then in the shape-note hymnal *Kentucky Harmony*, compiled in 1816 by Ananias Davisson. Tennessee was quick to follow Kentucky's lead with the 1818 publication of Alexander Johnson's *Johnson's Tennessee Harmony*. John B. Jackson published *The Knoxville Harmony* in 1838. Fa-sol-la singing (fasola), or shape-note singing, was practiced throughout Southern Appalachian church communities. Churches used this method in their hymnals. These hymnals allowed congregations with no musical training to participate in singing in harmony in a fully engaged fashion. The fasola shape-note singing utilized the pentatonic, or five-note, scale (the whole step "black notes" on the piano), eliminating the "leading tones" that are characteristic of keys and seven-note scales. Because there are no leading tones, the harmonization of a song using fasola possesses a distinct and modal sound. This significantly contributes to the unique character of songs sung using this system, and the resulting sound directly relates to the characterization of the harmony as a high lonesome sound that came to characterize bluegrass vocals.

# KENTUCKY HARMONY

OR

*A CHOICE COLLECTION OF PSALM TUNES, HYMNS, AND ANTHEMS.*

## IN THREE PARTS.

TAKEN FROM THE MOST EMINENT AUTHORS, AND WELL ADAPTED TO CHRISTIAN CHURCHES SINGING SCHOOLS, OR PRIVATE SOCIETIES.

### SELECTED BY

## A. DAVISSON.

PART I.

1816.

One shape-note singer using the doremi, or seven-note, shape-note system, gave the following account of his singing-school experience: "The books we used had seven different shapes, for notes, to represent the seven degrees of the scale, and no teacher I ever knew in those days would have recognized his favorite and best known song if he had seen it in 'round notes.' I had been to several singing-schools and, in fact, had about finished my musical education, before I ever heard of such a thing as 'round notes,' and the question was discussed throughout the country as to whether any man could possibly learn a new piece of music written in 'round notes.'"

In the South, singing schools were rural and recreational. Singing societies organized by churches contributed to the publication of a long list of hymnbooks and resources for group singing and instruction.

In the North, the European traditional practice of round-note notation prevailed, as well as a hymn tradition based on slow harmonic rhythms, parallel thirds and sixths, and the use of common major keys. This tradition, known as the Reformed or Progressive Movement, promoted musical instruction through public schools, choral societies, music normal institutes, and the publication of sacred, educational, and popular music. The South was more conservative and maintained the folk traditions and customs taught by the old, 18th-century singing schools. This tradition was characterized by rapid harmonic movement, parallel fourths and fifths, and minor and modal keys. Hymn notation in the South was characterized by the Character Notation Group (fasola and doremi). This method of music education was based on such pedagogical methods as letter and numerical notation, as well as four and seven shape-note tune books. In the North, hymnbook publications were rectangular; in the South, they were oblong. (RS.)

Some churches, such as the Primitive Baptist Church, did not promote the singing of hymns in harmony, although there is ample evidence that occasional harmony did occur. Gospel songbooks continued to be published in Tennessee in the mid-19th century. Composers and publishers, such as M.L. Swan, published songbooks, and later, song leaders and songwriters such as Homer Rodeheaver (1880–1955) emerged from traditional congregations and found a larger itinerant platform in the form of evangelistic crusades. Rodeheaver grew up learning mountain ballads and spirituals in Jellico, Tennessee, and later partnered with evangelist Billy Sunday to popularize a new form of religious song: the gospel song.

# Eight

# STARS ALIGN

Kentucky songwriter, mandolin player, and singer-performer Bill Monroe (1911–1996) became the reason for the association of this musical form with the term bluegrass. Monroe was known as a hillbilly string band leader as early as the 1930s. His family was from Rosine, Kentucky, which is relatively close to Appalachia and the Bluegrass region of Kentucky but, more accurately, is in the coalfield country of the western part of the state. Kentucky does include the Appalachian Mountain range in the east, as well as the bluegrass fields of Lexington and northern Kentucky, but both of these regions are many miles from Rosine. (AOA.)

In 1939, Bill Monroe, the "Father of Bluegrass Music," and his Blue Grass Boys made their Grand Ole Opry premiere at Nashville's War Memorial Auditorium, the original home of the iconic WSM radio show. Pictured is the Union Gospel Tabernacle, later known as Ryman Auditorium and home of the Grand Ole Opry. (TSL.)

Fiddler Chubby Wise joined with Bill Monroe in 1942 and formulated a new sound, which would lead to the sound that would eventually be known as bluegrass. The fiddle had been the foundation of mountain music for centuries. In one of his first major hit songs, Monroe writes and sings about his fiddling uncle, "Uncle Pen": "He played an old piece, he called 'Soldier's Joy' / And the one he called 'Boston Boy' / The greatest of all was 'Jenny Lynn' / To me that's where fidd'lin' began." Pictured is legendary fiddler Vassar Clements, who played with Monroe in the 1950s. (AOA.)

In Bill Monroe's autobiographical lyrics in "Uncle Pen," by listing "Soldier's Joy," "Boston Boy," and "Jenny Lynn," he is chronicling a group of fiddle tunes that had been passed down, along with musical customs, from one generation to another via oral tradition. Monroe, himself a "William" or "Billy" of the "Hill-Billy" lineage, along with every other folk musician before and after him, preserved these songs, ballads, and tunes from Scotch and Irish ancestors.

In "Uncle Pen," Monroe fuses fiddle classics with a distinctively new characteristic that would come to define bluegrass: clockwork precision rhythms, mesmerizing three-part harmony high in the male vocal range, and the "sing higher, play faster, perform louder" driving energy of the individual players. (LOC.)

Many popular hillbilly bands of Monroe's day adopted the five-instrument combination of fiddle, mandolin, banjo, guitar, and double bass. The well-known hillbilly group of Ralph and Carter Stanley and the Carter Family, both from Southwest Virginia, and Lester Flatt and Earl Scruggs, were all early contemporaries of Monroe. When Monroe combined forces with Flatt and Scruggs by inviting them to join his band, the Blue Grass Boys, lightning struck. Along with fiddler Chubby Wise and bass player Howard "Cedric Rainwater" Watts (both from Florida), Monroe's iconic voice, mandolin playing and songwriting combined with Scruggs's fast three-finger picking style of 16th note rolls and hammered appoggiatura on banjo and Flatt's pluck-and-strum rhythmic combination of bass note and harmony on guitar and rhythmic turnaround cadence figures to cement the sound that became bluegrass. The fiddle and double bass contributed just as significantly on the top and bottom of the sound spectrum to solidify the pillars of the bluegrass sound. Significantly, these three musicians—Monroe, Flatt, and Scruggs—were from Kentucky, Tennessee, and North Carolina, respectively. Pictured is the former Cleveland County courthouse in Shelby, North Carolina, which is now home to the Earl Scruggs Center. (LOC.)

# Nine
# Appalachia Takes to the Air

Audiences for bluegrass music during its early years consisted of blue-collar workers, farm families, and working-class folks in the rural Appalachian South. As the music became popular with middle-class urban folks, it started to grow and thrive as a distinct genre of its own. While folk and fiddle music was often associated with dancing, bluegrass was more of a concert presentation, with performances taking place on a stage. Although the instruments were acoustic, the band and the vocals for the band were dependent upon microphones, which helped shaped the sound of bluegrass and became the silent—but not *really* silent—instrument of the bluegrass ensemble. (AOA.)

WNOX Knoxville is one of the oldest radio stations in the United States. The station began broadcasting with 50 watts at 560 kilocycles in November 1921. In the days before television, the WNOX *Mid-Day Merry-Go-Round* featured early hillbilly, string band, folk, country, and bluegrass stars such as Archie Campbell, Chet Atkins and other performers. Additional stars who appeared on WNOX productions include Kitty Wells, Homer and Jethro, the Carter Family featuring June (Carter) Cash, Martha Carson, Roy Acuff, and Don Gibson. (AOA.)

The master of ceremonies for the programming of the WNOX *Saturday Night Barn Dance* was Lowell Blanchard, who came from Detroit to program a live hillbilly show and to audition talent. It was under Blanchard's direction that Homer and Jethro first dazzled audiences with their act and songs. Homer and Jethro epitomized the comedian act that accompanied early country and bluegrass shows and represented a direct carryover from the days of minstrelsy. (AOA.)

# Ten

# WHAT MAKES BLUEGRASS BLUEGRASS?

The music of Bill Monroe and his Blue Grass Boys was well known to Appalachian audiences. Performing with the Grand Ole Opry since 1939, their distinct high lonesome sound was broadcast over WSM radio in Nashville and could be heard on RCA Victor and Columbia Records. The National Life and Accident Insurance Company of Nashville began in 1900 as the National Sick and Accident Association. It later reorganized and adopted the National Life name. Known for its creative marketing development, National Life began WSM radio in 1923 as a result of the work of Edwin Craig, and it went on the air for the first time in 1925. As one of the earliest stations in radio broadcasting, WSM's call sign contained only three letters and was based on the company's insurance motto, "We Shield Millions." The birth of bluegrass was captured on Columbia's 1946/47 recordings of Bill Monroe and his original bluegrass band. (LOC.)

Bill Monroe and his Blue Grass Boys solidified the characteristics that define bluegrass as a genre and continued to define the sound of the bands that followed in their footsteps. (AOA.)

Characteristics unique to bluegrass include the combination of the mountain instruments of fiddle, banjo, guitar, mandolin, and bass; the shape-note voicing that included the high treble part above the melody (the "high lonesome sound") as a standard feature; the punctuated, added "turnaround" measure added before starting a new verse, including the classic G-Run; the frenetic, driving rhythmic pulse and undercurrent microrhythms; fast playing with laser accuracy and tuning; frequent use of open string tuning and keys; three part vocal harmony; unique rhythmic and melodic figures; the use of a single microphone for the amplification of acoustic instruments in performance and choreography around that single mic for solo breaks; a player/comedian band member, a carryover from minstrelsy; antihillbilly professional dress for a contrasting appearance; recurring narrative themes and words such as cabin, woods, mother, train, farewell, lonesome, valley, rambling, death, hills, mountains, river, Kentucky, Tennessee, grave, whiskey, marrying, murder, and the subjects of love and unrequited love; and use of the words "family," "boys," and "ramblers" in the names of the bands, as in Blue Grass Boys, Clinch Mountain Boys, Foggy Mountain Boys, Smoky Mountain Boys, Sunny Mountain Boys, and, as caricatured in the film *O Brother, Where Art Thou?*, the fictitious Soggy Bottom Boys.

The youth following of Earl Scruggs and his banjo was launched in 1959 when he appeared with Joan Baez and Pete Seeger at the first Newport Folk Festival. TV shows and motion pictures romanticized and exaggerated hillbilly and rural stereotypes and created caricatures of early mountain, hillbilly, and bluegrass notions. They also further popularized the music of the mountains and bluegrass performers. Following the success of the early radio shows, broadcast television created rural comedies such as *The Andy Griffith Show* (1960–1968), *The Beverly Hillbillies* (1962–1971), *Green Acres* (1965–1971), and *Petticoat Junction* (1963–1970) to capitalize on an American fascination with rural and mountain life. The careers of Flatt and Scruggs, the Dillards (the Darlings of *The Andy Griffith Show*), and Ralph Stanley, among others, were advanced because of this extraordinary media attention throughout the 1960s. (AOA.)

Roy Acuff and his Smoky Mountain boys with Rachel

STRINGBEAN
"THE KENTUCKY WONDER"
25 YEARS WITH THE GRAND OLE OPRY

Motion pictures such as *Bonnie and Clyde* (1967), featuring Earl Scruggs's "Foggy Mountain Breakdown"; *Deliverance* (1972), featuring the song "Dueling Banjos"; and other films, such as *O Brother, Where Art Thou?* (2000) and *Songcatcher* (2000), brought Appalachian and bluegrass music even further into the mainstream. Telling the stories of early-20th-century songcatchers such as Childs, Campbell, Sharp, and Karpeles, the movie *Songcatcher* showed migrated mountain ballads to a new audience using the best of country and folk recording artists. Using the mythology of the Delta blues, the film *O Brother, Where Art Thou?* featured traditional American folk and bluegrass songs and spirituals such as "I Sought My Lord in the Wilderness," "Down to the Valley to Pray" ("River"), the shape-note hymn "Angel Band," and the Stanley Brothers' "Man of Constant Sorrow," first published by Dick Burnett, a partially blind fiddler from Kentucky. "Man of Constant Sorrow" was originally titled "Farewell Song" in a songbook by Burnett dated around 1913. (AOA.)

There are additional unique characteristics related to the sound, style, and performance of bluegrass music. A listener and observer can find these attributes at play in classic and contemporary bluegrass performances, which can all be traced back—in one form or another—to the earliest examples of bluegrass. (LOC.)

Bluegrass performance on stage is competitive: sing higher, play faster, perform louder, and, in general, play hotter and better than the other guy—but it has to be done in a way that complements the group's overall sound and style, and one must feign humility. This factor alone may account for the exciting dynamic and drive of the bluegrass ensemble. The musicians play off of and push each other creatively and aggressively. In contrast, most old-time and country music was relatively laid back in comparison. (AOA.)

The competitive spirit in bluegrass primarily came from Bill Monroe, who put old-time music into overdrive. He drove the players with his mandolin and pushed them as he played on top of the beat. This characteristic still defines bluegrass today. Contemporary bluegrass musicians such as Ricky Skaggs and Del McCoury demonstrate this drive. (AOA.)

Bluegrass music is a social medium—bluegrass served as a means for social interaction among rural folks. People played music together as a way to provide fellowship and entertainment, and this phenomenon continues today among those who participate in this form of music-making. (LOC.)

Even in the early days of bluegrass, pros would jam with fans at festivals and in homes. Long before YouTube, most musicians would willingly share what they were doing, what they knew, and how they did what they did. The author recalls one day when he was playing banjo on the front porch and a car slowed down in front of the house, pulled over, and the driver got out of the car with his guitar, walked up to the porch, sat down, and his only words were: "You lead." (AOA.)

The instrumentation for bluegrass is unique—fiddle, mandolin, banjo, guitar, and upright bass are the defining instruments. Bill Monroe defined and solidified the genre. Sally Ann "Wilene" Forrester (also called "Billie") played accordion with Monroe very early on, but he dropped the instrument after she left his band in 1945. Flatt and Scruggs added a dobro to their configuration, an instrument that complements the sound of the classic instrumentation, but the dobro remains a "cousin" to the bluegrass family rather than a sibling. (LOC.)

The escalating intensity of the timbre, or unique color of tone each instrument produces, is significant to the "faster, louder, higher, better" formula at work in a bluegrass configuration. Although none of the instruments can be compared in terms of faster, louder, higher, or better, they can all provide an escalation of brightness and intensity of sound. This is very clear when it comes to the need for amplification. (LOC.)

The instruments most in need of amplification would likely be ranked in this order from mellow to intense: guitar, mandolin, bass and fiddle, and, finally, banjo. Each instrument represents a heightened level of intensity of sound in the timbre and overtone spectrum. (LOC.)

There is no bluegrass without virtuosity—old-time and string band music was more like hillbilly chamber music, with standout exceptions being Clayton McMichen and Uncle Dave Macon. From the beginning, bluegrass featured soloists on banjo, fiddle, and mandolin, while the rest of the band added a rhythmic nest and backed up the solo breaks. (LOC.)

Bluegrass has been likened to baseball in terms of how Bill Monroe loved and carried a team with his tent shows in the 1940s—when the time comes for one performer's solo in a song, they are up to bat and need to hit it out of the park. Earl Scruggs epitomized the out-of-the-park solo in his role with Bill Monroe's Blue Grass Boys. (LOC.)

Phrasing and solos are determined by the single microphone; when there is a hole in the phrase of a bluegrass song, a soloist will fill that space. These fills, as they are called, are individualistic. You will hear vamping in different places in the music where nothing much is happening except beating the time. The players will individually fill those holes with improvisation at the end of the melody line. This developed because in the early days of bluegrass, there was only one microphone, and each player had to wait for the fiddler or banjo player to get out of the way so the singer could come back to the microphone. (LOC.)

Movement around the mic appears almost like choreography during a bluegrass performance. The added measure at the end of the verse of a bluegrass song is there to allow for this movement to take place after the verse ends. The interesting aspect of this stylistic feature is that even when every instrument is amplified and there is no shuffling around a single mic, the added measure remains in the performance of the song. (AOA.)

Classic fills and signature rhythmic/melodic figures at the end of a phrase are Lester Flatt's significant and enduring contributions to the bluegrass sound and the guitar's rhythmic contribution to the ensemble. His name is often mentioned alongside the "G-Run" (pictured on page 102). This distinctive run is heard in practically every traditional bluegrass song that can be played on the guitar using a G chord. In its original form, it is basically a six-note run played at the end of a verse or chorus. It punctuates the song and serves the same purpose as an exclamation point at the end of a paragraph, leading to the conclusion or cadence of a verse or the entire song. (LOC.)

Lester Flatt's G-Run can be traced back at least as far as the mid-1930s, when Riley Puckett played a version of it on the August 8, 1935, recording of "Blue Ridge Mountain Blues." On June 15, 1936, Zeke Morris played his version of the guitar run when he and Wade Mainer recorded "If I Can Hear My Mother Pray Again." Listening closely to Bill and Charlie Monroe's October 12, 1936, recording of "Roll in My Sweet Baby's Arms," one can hear Charlie playing something that approaches the Lester Flatt G-Run. (LOC.)

On November 25, 1939, in Bill Monroe's first appearance on *Grand Ole Opry*, Monroe amazed the audience with his performance of Jimmie Rodgers's song "Mule Skinner Blues." For this number, Blue Grass Boy Cleo Davis chorded Monroe's mandolin, and Bill played guitar and used a run similar to the Lester Flatt G-Run. Monroe also played the run when he recorded this song with the Blue Grass Boys on October 7, 1940, for RCA Victor Records. If there is a genome for bluegrass music, the G-Run is it. (LOC.)

Additional stylistic patterns heard in bluegrass include the hammering on a string when a finger strikes a string that is already playing and the pulling off of a string, which creates a two-note rhythm—both techniques add yet another sound to the already packed single beat of the music. These generally occur at the end of a phrase such as the hammered turnaround of the five-note pentatonic of "do, re-mi, sol-la, do" run and its variations. (LOC.)

Another run used only to conclude a song at the final cadence is a descending arpeggio pattern in which the tonic note is played multiple times in syncopation, then descends to the hammered notes of the chord and, finally, to the root of the harmony. Blues and chromatic versions of these runs and other variations abound. (LOC.)

A percussive accompaniment figure on the backbeat is a standard rhythmic feature in bluegrass music. These strokes across the strings are called chucks because of the muted and percussive sound they make on muted strings played on backbeats as chords or simply as percussive strokes to the full spread of the strings.

# ORIGINAL SACRED HARP

## DENSON REVISION
## 1971 EDITION

The Best Collection of Sacred Songs, Hymns, Odes, and
Anthems Ever Offered the Singing Public for General Use

## MUSIC COMMITTEE

Hugh McGraw, Chairman  
Mrs. Ruth Denson Edwards, Secretary  
Palmer Godsey  
Foy Frederick  
Elder Elmer Kitchens  
Walter A. Parker  

Consultants: Dr. William J. Reynolds and Dr. Emory S. Bucke

Copyright © 1971 by Sacred Harp Publishing Company, Inc., Cullman, Alabama.
All rights reserved. International copyright secured.

Printed by the Kingsport Press
Kingsport, Tennessee

Bluegrass was originally regional music—it grew out of the Southern Appalachian mountain music and the musical experience found across the Southeast. This flavored the language, subject matter, vocal phrasings, and tempos of the songs being performed.

There was a time when you could tell where someone was from by the way they played and sang. In the words of Doc Watson, "Back in the days before the media came into play, even before the Victrola, each hollow had its own version of a ballad." (LOC.)

In the mid-20th century, bluegrass spread throughout the country as Appalachian and southern people migrated north and west looking for work, taking their music with them. Bluegrass is performed worldwide but is still most prevalent in the southeastern United States.

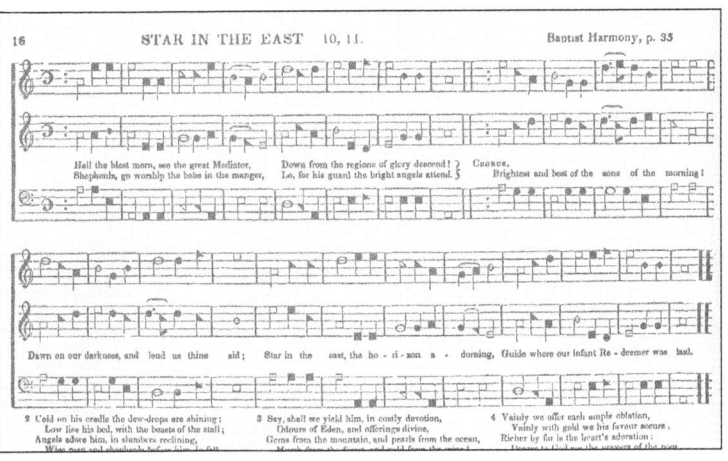

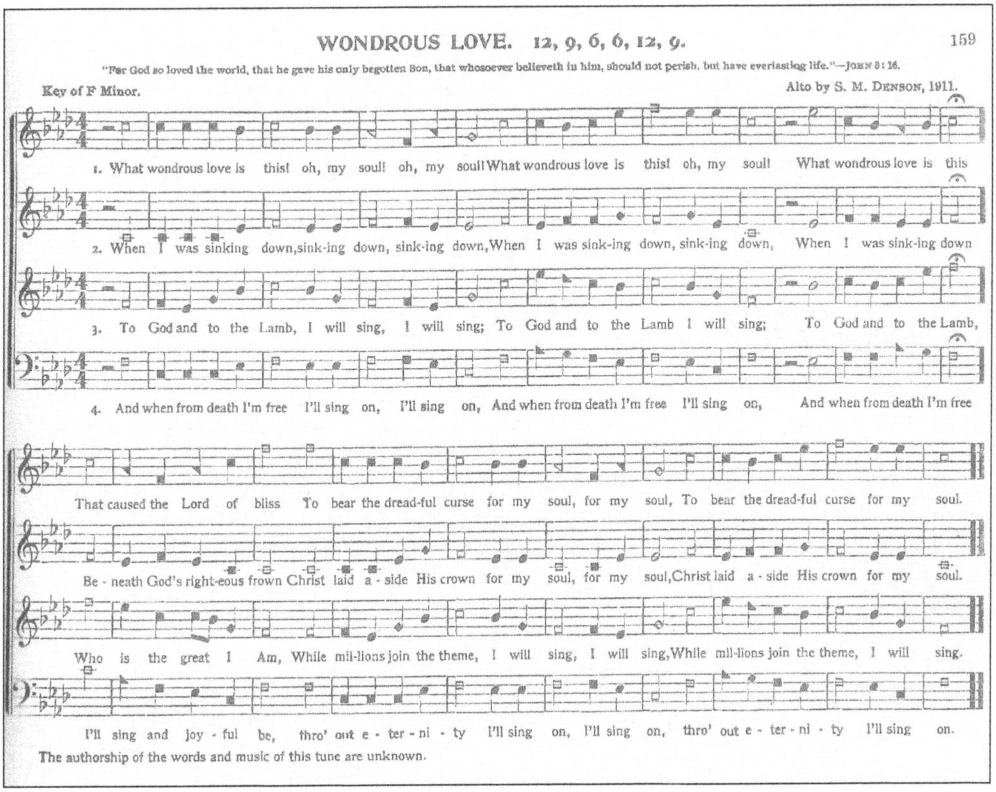

Bluegrass may never be a musical genre that appeals to the masses. It is a rural form existing in an increasingly urban environment. The mountain images and lonesome themes and sound of bluegrass may diminish as shared experiences as society moves more and more toward cities and urbanization.

To some, bluegrass songs may sound similar, making it hard to sustain interest—unless, of course, you play one of the bluegrass instruments. Society has changed, but bluegrass most likely will not. (FDS.)

However, the bluegrass songs that have emerged and remain with us, the performance style that mesmerizes us, and the new songs that carry the bluegrass sound and bear the fundamental characteristics of classic bluegrass style will continue to take us to a place we want to go—back to East Tennessee, like a perfect mountain vacation. (LOC.)

# BIBLIOGRAPHY

Bartenstein, Fred, ed. *Bluegrass Bluesman Josh Graves: A Memoir*. Chicago: University of Illinois Press, 2012.
Becker, Jane S. *Selling Tradition: Appalachia and the Construction of an American Folk, 1930–1940*. Chapel Hill: University of North Carolina Press, 1998.
Biggers, Jeff. *The United States of Appalachia: How Southern Mountaineers Brought Independence, Culture, and Enlightenment to America*. Berkeley, CA: Counterpoint, 2006.
Campbell, Olive Dame. *Appalachian Travels: The Diary of Olive Dame Campbell*. Edited by Elizabeth McCutchen Williams. Lexington: University of Kentucky Press, 2012.
———. *The Life and Work of John Charles Campbell, September 15, 1868–May 2, 1919*. Madison, WI: College Printing, 1968.
Chadwick, Nora. *The Celts*. New York: Penguin Books, 1971.
Cheesman, Tom, and Sigrid Rieuwerts. *Ballads into Books: The Legacy of Francis James Child*. Edited by Peter Lang. Bern, Switzerland: Cheesman & Rieuwerts, 1997.
Deaderick, Lucile, ed. *Heart of the Valley: A History of Knoxville, Tennessee*. Knoxville: East Tennessee Historical Society, 1976.
Doyle, David Noel, and Owen Dudley Edwards. *America and Ireland 1776–1976: The American Identity and the Irish Connection: The Proceedings of the United States Bicentennial Conference of Cumann Merriman*. Ennis, Westport, Ireland: Greenwood Press, 1980.
Eller, Ronald D. *Miners, Millhands, and Mountaineers: Industrialization of the Appalachian South, 1880–1930*. Knoxville: University of Tennessee Press, 1982.
Ferris, Jean. *America's Musical Landscape*. New York: McGraw-Hill, 2002.
Garreau, Joel. *The Nine Nations of North America*. New York: Avon Books, 1981.
Goldsmith, Thomas, ed. *The Bluegrass Reader*. Chicago: University of Illinois Press, 2004.
Havighurst, Craig. *Air Castle of the South: WSM and the Making of Music City*. Chicago: University of Illinois Press, 2007.
Kennedy, Billy. *The Scotch-Irish in the Hills of Tennessee*. Belfast: Ambassador Productions, 1995.
Montgomery, Michael. "How Scotch-Irish is your English?" *Journal of East Tennessee History*, no. 77.
Nettl, Bruno. *Folk Music in the United States: An Introduction*. Detroit, MI: Wayne State University Press, 1976.
O'Neal, Patricia. *Room at the Foot of the Bed*. Lexington, KY: self-published, 1991.
Pinson, Bob, compiler. *The Bristol Sessions: Historic Recordings from Bristol, Tennessee*. Nashville: Country Music Foundation, 1991.
Putnam, A.W. *History of Middle Tennessee; Or, Life and Times of Gen. James Roberston*. Nashville: self-published, 1859.
Rosenberg, Neil V. *Bluegrass: A History*. Chicago: University of Illinois Press, 1993.
Scott, Christian. *Ralph Peer's The Bristol Sessions: An Illustrated Discography*. R. Lees, 2016.
Sharp, Cecil J., and Maud Karpeles, with Specimen piano accompaniment by Benjamin Britten. *Eighty English Folk Songs*. London: Faber and Faber, 1968.
Sharp, Tim. *Memphis Music before the Blues*. Charleston, SC: Arcadia Publishing, 2007.
———. *Nashville Music before Country*. Charleston, SC: Arcadia Publishing, 2008.
Smith, Richard D. *Can't You Hear Me Callin': The Life of Bill Monroe, Father of Bluegrass*. Cambridge, MA: Da Capo Press, 2001.
Stanley, Ralph. *Man of Constant Sorrow: My Life and Times*. New York: Gotham Books, 2009.

Still, James. *River of Earth*. Lexington: University of Kentucky Press, 1978.
Sutton, Brett. "Shape-Note Tune Books and Primitive Hymns." *Ethnomusicology* 26, no. 1 (January 1982): 11–26.
Vance, J.D. *Hillbilly Elegy*. New York: HarperCollins, 2016.
Weisberger, Bernard A. *They Gathered at the River*. Boston: Little, Brown, 1958.
Yates, Mike, Elaine Bradtke, Malcolm Taylor, and Shirley Collins. *Dear Companion: Appalachian Traditional Songs and Singers from the Cecil Sharp Collection*. London: English Folk Dance & Song Society, 2004.
Zimmerman, Peter Coats. *Tennessee Music: Its People and Places*. San Francisco: Miller Freeman Books, 1998.

# INDEX

Acuff, Roy, 100
Allen, William Frances, 56
Atkins, Chet (Chester Burton), 100
Baez, Joan, 103
ballad, 2, 7, 15, 30, 31, 33, 36, 37, 42–47, 49–55, 59, 62, 64, 65, 69, 70, 85, 94, 97, 103, 123
Billings, William, 89
Blanchard, Lowell, 100
Blount, William, 39
Blue Grass Boys, the, 7, 56, 74, 75, 80, 87, 96–98, 101, 102, 113, 118
Bristol, 7, 11, 52, 68–72
Bumgarner, Samantha, 79
Burnett, Dick (Richard Daniel), 103
Campbell, Archie, 100
Campbell, John, 45, 46
Campbell, Olive Dame, 44–47, 51, 54, 103
Carson, Martha, 100
Carter, A.P., 27, 28, 70
Carter Family, 28, 69, 70, 98, 100
Carter, Maybelle, 28, 70
Carter, Sara, 28, 70
Cash, June (Carter), 27, 100
Cherokee, 13, 16, 17, 37
Child, Frances James, 44, 103
Clinton, George, 37
Columbia Records, 101
Craig, Edwin, 101
Davis, Cleo, 118
Davisson, Ananias, 91
Flatt, Lester, 80, 83, 87, 98, 103, 109, 116–118
Forrester, Sally Ann "Wilene," 109
Gamble, James, 41
Garrison, Lucy McKim, 56

Gibson, Don, 100
Gililand, Henry C., 67
Grand Ole Opry, 7, 11, 83, 96, 101, 118
Graves, "Uncle" Josh, 80
Heinemann, Otto K.E., 68
hillbilly, 2, 33, 35, 66, 67, 88, 95, 97, 98, 100, 103, 112
Homer and Jethro, 100
Jackson, George Pullen, 55
Jackson, John B., 91
Jim and Jesse, 87
Johnson, Alexander, 91
Karpeles, Maud, 7, 47, 48, 50, 51, 53, 54, 59, 103
Kentucky Thunder, 87
Knox, Henry, 37, 39
Knoxville, 7, 11, 13, 15, 16, 18, 37, 39, 40, 48
Krauss, Alison, 87
Law, Andrew, 91
Little, William, 91
lonesome, 51, 55–62, 66, 83, 85, 87, 89, 91, 101, 102, 124
Macon, Uncle Dave, 112
Mariner, Wade, 117
McCoury, Del (Delano Floyd), 106
McMichen, Clayton, 112
Monroe, Bill, 7, 56, 74, 75, 80, 83, 87, 89, 95–98, 101, 102, 106, 109, 113, 117, 118
Monroe, Charlie, 117
Morris, Zeke, 117
Newport Folk Festival, 103
OKeh Record Company, 7, 68
Parton, Dolly, 54
Peer, Ralph, 68, 69, 71
Puckett, Riley, 117
Putnam, A.W., 41
RCA Victor, 7, 67, 101, 118
Robertson, Eck (Alexander Campbell), 67

Rodeheaver, Homer, 94
Rodgers, Jimmie, 69–71, 87, 118
Rosenberg, Neil, 75
Scotch-Irish, 14, 15, 25, 26, 31–35, 37, 38, 69, 86, 88, 97
Scruggs, Earl, 77, 80, 83, 87, 98, 103, 109, 113
Seeger, Pete, 103
shape note, 86, 90–93, 102, 103
Sharp, Cecil J., 7, 45, 47–52, 54, 55, 57, 59, 65, 103
singing school, 89–93
Skaggs, Ricky, 87, 106
Smith, Ada, 46
Smith, William, 91
Stanley, Carter, 58, 98
Stanley, Ralph, 66, 87, 88, 98, 103
Stoneman, "Pop" Ernest, 68
Sunday, Billy, 94
Swan, M.L., 94
Sweeney, Joel, 77
Ulster (Irish), 14, 25, 26, 32, 33, 36, 37
Victor Talking Machine Company, 67, 71
Ware, Charles Pickard, 56
Watson, Doc (Arthel Lane), 123
Watts, Cedric Rainwater (Howard), 98
Watts, Isaac, 89
Webb, Robert, 79
Webster, J.P., 70
Wells, Kitty, 100
White, James, 39
Wise, Chubby (Robert Russell), 96, 98
WNOX, 100
WSM Radio, 7, 11, 96, 101

Visit us at
arcadiapublishing.com

www.ingramcontent.com/pod-product-compliance
Lightning Source LLC
Chambersburg PA
CBHW060922170426
43191CB00025B/2461